W9-ARK-212

MARGARET THATCHER

Britain's Prime Minister

Dorothy Hole

—*Contemporary Women Series*—

ENSLOW PUBLISHERS, INC.

Bloy St. & Ramsey Ave.   P.O. Box 38
Box 777   Aldershot
Hillside, N.J. 07205   Hants GU12 6BP
U.S.A.   U.K.

Library of Congress Cataloging-in-Publication Data

Hole, Dorothy.
    Margaret Thatcher, Britain's prime minister.
    (Contemporary women series)

    Includes bibliographical references.

    Summary: Presents the life of Britain's first woman prime minister and describes her influence on worldwide politics.

    1. Thatcher, Margaret—Juvenile literature. 2. Prime ministers—Great Britain—Biography—Juvenile literature. 3. Great Britain—Politics and government—1979– —Juvenile literature. 4. Women prime ministers—Great Britain—Biography—Juvenile literature. [1. Thatcher, Margaret. 2. Prime ministers] I. Title. II. Series.

DA591.T47H64 1990 941.085'8' 092 [B] [92] 89-16996

ISBN 0-89490-246-6

Printed in the United States of America

10 9 8 7 6 5 4 3 2 1

Illustration Credits: Courtesy of
Gerald R. Ford Library, pp. 46, 78; No. 10 Downing Street, p. 120; The Press Association Ltd., pp. 16, 22, 30, 39, 54, 62, 70, 86, 94; Ronald Reagan Presidential Materials Staff, p. 104; The White House (David Valdez), p. 112.

Cover Photo: Courtesy of No. 10 Downing Street

Contents

to Mac

Acknowledgments

The author wishes to thank the following for their invaluable assistance: Edwina Iredale, Librarian, British Consulate, Los Angeles; Janet Jenks, Head, Humanities & Social Science Library, California Institute of Technology, Pasadena; Alma Feuerabendt and Nancy Brown, Assistants to Janet Jenks.

UNITED KINGDOM

SCOTLAND

N. IRELAND

IRELAND

ENGLAND

WALES

"Politics was in my bloodstream."

1

No. 10 Downing Street in London is one of the most famous addresses in the world. Since 1735, it has been the official residence of Britain's prime minister, the equivalent of our president. And only one woman has ever held that position: Margaret Thatcher.

The younger of the two daughters of Alfred and Beatrice Roberts, Margaret Hilda was born on October 13, 1925, in a small apartment where she lived until she went to college. It was located above her father's grocery store in the market town of Grantham, 105 miles north of London.

Margaret was a thoughtful child with a round face, blue eyes, and the same lovely complexion she has today. She soon showed that she had an exceptionally fine brain. A former school friend, John Foster, says, "She was bright, studious, serious even as a five-year old."

Her stern maternal grandmother lived with them. She preached cleanliness and work as the two major virtues. For Margaret and her sister, home life revolved around study and religion. Her father's personality dominated the family, and from an early age, Margaret adored him. Many, many years later, as she entered No. 10 Downing Street for the first time as prime minister, she told the world, "I owe almost everything to my father." *Quote*

The oldest of a shoemaker's seven children, Alfred Roberts had dropped out of school when he was twelve years old. He "had a passion for education," Margaret Thatcher says, and wanted his children to receive the education he had been denied. He found a job in a grocery store in Grantham. He later met Beatrice Stephenson, a seamstress, whom he eventually married. Beatrice's father was a machinist and her mother a railway station cloakroom attendant.

Both Alfred and Beatrice were hard workers and believed in saving their earnings. Soon Alfred was able to open his own grocery store, where Beatrice helped him. In 1921 Muriel was born, with Margaret's birth following four years later.

Their apartment was barely adequate. Washing was done with a jug of water and a basin at the bedroom washstand. There was no hot water, inside toilet, or garden, and only a tiny kitchen. The weekly bath involved lugging pails of hot water heated on the stove to a tub in the warehouse at the back of the store.

But Beatrice and her two girls kept their home "as bright as a new pin," Margaret remembers. She and her sister were expected to help with the housework, which even included painting the walls.

Their furniture was dark mahogany wood, heavy and ornate, most of it secondhand. The main piece was the piano. From the age of five, Margaret took piano lessons, her musical ability inherited from her mother. It is claimed that Margaret could have become a concert pianist. However, when she was fifteen, she decided to concentrate on schoolwork and gave up studying the piano.

In Britain, education was compulsory for ages five to fourteen (now sixteen). The same year Margaret started her music instruction, she was enrolled in Huntingtower Street Elementary School. Eager to learn, Margaret was a model student, helped by an overwhelming desire to please her father. For his part, Alf Roberts was not above "pushing" her in her studies. Margaret later admitted, "He did try to realize his ambition in me."

8

Margaret had no social life outside the church, for her father was a serious-minded, religious man. With her family, she attended the Finkin Street Methodist Church, where she participated in various events such as church socials, singalongs, and spelling bees. On Sunday, Margaret and her sister walked to Finkin Street four times—twice to Sunday School, twice to services.

Margaret gave her pennies to church missions and was urged by her parents to do things for those less fortunate. Her mother set an example by baking more bread than the family could eat, to give to the needy.

"We were always encouraged to think in terms of practical help," Margaret says. "The crucial thing was what you were prepared to do, yourself, out of your own slender income."

Margaret never brought a friend home from school; she never played games after school. It wasn't until elementary school, when she saw the fun other children had, that she realized there was more to life than work, study, and religion. When she asked her father about the activities of her classmates, he said, "Never do things or want to do things just because other people do them. Make up your own mind about what you are going to do and persuade people to go your way."

This advice still lives with Margaret Thatcher. Her political career demonstrates that she took his words to heart.

One activity was encouraged: reading. As soon as Margaret was old enough, she began walking to the library once a week to collect books for the family. Her father enjoyed biographies and current events, which, as she grew older, were Margaret's choice, too. They held lengthy discussions about the nonfiction works. In Alfred Roberts' mind, his daughters automatically were interested in whatever interested him. In this way, Margaret's knowledge became greater than that of most of her classmates. Margaret believes she received a good education not only in school but at home as well.

"I always got the books I wanted but no pleasures," Margaret recalls. "I never went to a dance until I got to university."

The family as a group also went to university extension lectures, musicals, and anything else that Alfred thought would add to his children's—and his own—education.

Beatrice Roberts seems to have been a quiet woman who spent her days helping in the store, keeping house, and baking; her one outside interest was a sewing group that met at the church on Wednesday evening. Intellectually, she did not keep up with her husband's expanding horizons.

Each of the family members worked in the store. Margaret helped by waiting on customers. She placed items on shelves, weighed and packaged products (everything from sugar to dried fruits to jam) that were shipped in bulk to the Roberts' store. She remembers that "it was quite a big shop. . . . A lot of people came in . . . and knowing we were all interested in what was going on in the world, we would talk quite late."

Because the store was open for ten to twelve hours every day but Sunday and either Mr. or Mrs. Roberts always had to be there, the family rarely sat down to a meal together. In England, especially in the small towns, the stores close early one afternoon a week. In Grantham, early closing day was Thursday. Once in a while, Margaret received permission to leave school on Thursday to go to the movies with her parents, because holidays were the only times they could do things together. Even vacations were taken at different times. Mrs. Roberts and the girls enjoyed one week of sea air and sun at Skegness on the North Sea, and Mr. Roberts spent a week there alone later on.

Eventually Margaret's father saved enough to buy a second store. Busy as he was with his two stores, his church (he was a lay preacher), and his family, Alfred Roberts still found time for community affairs. He was elected to the Grantham Borough Council and served for twenty-five years. He was also a part-time justice of the peace and eventually became mayor of Grantham. Political discussions were a way of life for the Roberts family, so Margaret learned firsthand a great deal about politics. She once told an interviewer that by the time she was ten, "Politics was in my bloodstream."

Her first active role in a political campaign happened when she was ten. Thrilled at her assignment, she carried the lists of those who had voted from the polling place to the candidates' head-quarters. At the headquarters, the names were crossed off the master list, permitting the staff to keep track of who had voted.

This same year, 1936, Margaret received a scholarship to Kesteven and Grantham Girls' School, the equivalent of a combined junior and senior high in the United States. Many students took the highly competitive entrance exam, for not only did the school have an excellent reputation, but it qualified as a "grant-aid" school. The government paid half the tuition, the parents the other half. But because of the scholarship, Margaret's parents did not have to pay anything. Her sister, Muriel, was already on scholarship there.

Margaret's school career at Kesteven was outstanding. A hard worker, she listened carefully in class and then went home and studied. Her diligence resulted in her being first in her class every year except one, when she came in second. Art was the one subject that brought down her average.

Former headmistress Dorothy Gillies believed that Margaret "had the ability to think clearly, tackling one thing at a time." School reports declared, "She is a very logical thinker."

Margaret herself maintains, "We were Methodists and Methodist means method." She went on to say, "We were taught what was right and wrong in considerable detail. There were certain things you just didn't do and that was that. Duty was very, very strongly ingrained into us." And a girl on scholarship had the obligation to study and do well.

Like so many good students, she proved an all-around athlete, hockey being her speciality. Before she left Kesteven, she had been vice captain of the hockey team and "captain of games," an honor that included representing Kesteven at interscholastic meets.

One of her closest friends, Margaret Edwards Hellaby, claims that people get the wrong idea about Margaret Thatcher, assuming her to have been a grind. "But she was also good at games, pretty, and popular."

When Margaret was thirteen, Muriel decided to become a physiotherapist. She moved to Birmingham to take her training. The same year, 1939, World War II began.

Soon Britain experienced a shortage of food and clothing. Everything had to be utilized. To help the war effort, Margaret and her friends picked rose hips. After the rose flower dies, a fruit, called a rose hip or rose apple, frequently grows. Because it contains vitamins, which were urgently needed in England at that time, it was made into a syrup. The girls also collected wool from bushes that sheep had brushed against. The wool was then used to make clothing.

Living in Grantham became unsafe. Its nearby military installations, its factories converted to manufacturing munitions, and its important railroads turned the town into a major German target. It is said to have had the highest ratio of bombs per person to fall on any town in Britain.

One exciting day, Margaret stood with the other students in a cloakroom, thought to be safer than other rooms because the window was reinforced with wire, while an enemy plane unloaded its bombs one by one across the hockey field, stopping just short of the main building. At home, when an air raid warning sounded, she would crawl under the dining room table.

Something else happened to Margaret during these years that opened her eyes to human rights and the tragedy to individuals when these rights are taken away by force. Muriel had a pen pal in Vienna, a young Jewish girl named Edith. When the Nazis stormed into Austria, her family feared for her safety. They wrote to Mr. and Mrs. Roberts. If Edith could be successfully gotten out of Austria, would they take her in? The Roberts immediately said yes, Edith could come and live with them.

From Edith, Margaret heard firsthand of the horrors of living under Hitler. The stories the young Jewish girl told gave Margaret a clearer idea of why Britain was fighting. She has never forgotten those stories.

The school Margaret attended was quite different from those in the United States. The final year, called VIth (Sixth) Form, could be taken three times: Lower Sixth, Higher Sixth, and then a final year that was usually attended by girls planning to go on to a university. Sixth Form is equivalent to twelfth grade in the United States.

Largely because of a wonderful teacher, Miss Kay, Margaret decided on chemistry as her university major. "One knew then," she says, "that science was the coming thing."

She frequently visited the courtroom where her father was presiding as justice of the peace. As time went by, she realized that law interested her more than chemistry, but she felt that her second year of Sixth Form was too late to switch her intended major at the university.

One day she ate lunch with her father and Norman Winning, the town's recorder (a town official who also serves as a part-time judge). She expressed her doubts about becoming a chemist. Mr. Winning was the perfect person to tell, for he had "read" (the English term for majoring in a subject) physics before becoming a lawyer.

He advised her to stick to her chemistry and after earning her degree, to go on to law. Many legal fields, he said, were open to a person with both a scientific and a legal background (such as patent law). Margaret decided to continue in chemistry.

She wanted to go to Somerville College at Oxford University.

The war had made young people eager to get on with life, and Margaret did not want to spend another year at Kesteven. "She was very ambitious," says her good friend Margaret Wickstead, "and wanted to go to university as fast as she could."

Unfortunately, Margaret Roberts had not taken Latin, a required subject for entrance to Oxford. Kesteven had not offered that subject until Dorothy Gillies, a classics scholar, became headmistress. By then Margaret had immersed herself in science courses, having no time on her schedule for Latin.

Miss Gillies believed Margaret at seventeen was too young to go to a university; that plus no Latin seemed to decide the matter.

"You're thwarting my ambition!" Margaret is supposed to have raged.

With her father's support, she undertook to cram four years of Latin into a few months, and she succeeded in doing so! She was already studying for a Higher School Certificate, and this made the work load tremendous.

She took the university entrance exam and, to her distress, did not get a high enough score to be accepted immediately. Her name was put on the waiting list.

Discouraged, she returned to Kesteven. Two weeks later, a telegram arrived. An unexpected opening had occurred, and the place was hers.

When Margaret left Grantham for Oxford, she took with her certain beliefs: hard work, serious study, doing for oneself, and doing one's duty.

Margaret Roberts was now on her way to making history.

Miss Margaret Roberts became active in politics during her college days at Oxford University in the early 1940s.

2

In 1943 Margaret settled down in a dormitory, Penrose Hall, in Oxford, a bustling university town. With its theaters, shops, concerts, and bookstores—so different from Grantham—Oxford opened up new worlds for the just-arrived Margaret Roberts. Even World War II had not stopped the students' activities.

At first homesick and shy, the eighteen-year-old found it difficult to make friends. Fortunately for her, studies filled her day. The alarm clock went off at 6:30 A.M. She spent her mornings and afternoons in the laboratory, and when her lab work for the day was done, Margaret attended lectures, usually from five until seven. Then she tackled the required reading.

Her tutor (a special professor assigned to help, instruct, and follow a student's academic progress) was Dorothy Hodgkin. (Dr. Hodgkin was to win the Nobel Prize for chemistry in 1964.) She later said that, although Margaret's work was nice and clear, she did not have a "particularly profound interest" in chemistry.

For the first time in her life, Margaret was able to participate in outside activities not connected with the church. Next to politics, her first interest was music. She joined three different groups: the Oxford Repertory Company, the Somerville-Balliol Choir, and the Bach Choir. The Scientific Society took up Friday evenings, and, probably to please her father, she became a member of the Methodist student organization. Most important, she became active in politics.

Although famous for its scholarship, Oxford University has always been a hotbed of political activity. The student body holds every kind of political belief imaginable: Socialist, Communist, Liberal, Labour, and Conservative, as well as lesser-known varieties. When Margaret entered the university she was a Conservative, and nothing happened to make her change her mind. If anything, the debates with her fellow students merely confirmed her beliefs.

It was natural for her to join the Oxford University Conservative Association (OUCA), and after that, Margaret's social life took off: teas, cocktail parties, and dances filled whatever free time she had. With her lovely blue eyes, beautiful complexion, and intelligent conversation, she was always popular. Once, she wanted to preserve a carnation given to her by a date. Margaret Goodwich Wickstead tells of Margaret Roberts' determined search through chemistry books looking for the right formula. Finally she had to give up and use aspirin and water!

Margaret moved to "digs," or a rooming house, for her third year. One of the other girls, Pauline Cowan, was as active for the Communists as Margaret was for the Conservatives. They were friendly, ate meals together, and had heated discussions. However, each remained convinced she was right and didn't make the slightest impression on the other.

By the time of the 1945 election, Margaret was well known for her work with the OUCA. She campaigned for Quintin Hogg, the Conservative candidate from Oxford to the House of Commons.

The central government of Britain is led by the prime minister and other departmental heads (called ministers), who form the Cabinet. Parliament is the supreme legislative body and consists of two houses: the House of Commons and the House of Lords.

The House of Commons is Britain's real governing body. The members are elected in a general election, which must be held at least every five years, but which may be called anytime. The prime minister and most ministers sit in the House of Commons, where they explain and define their policies and answer questions at "Question Time."

Membership in the House of Lords is inherited along with a title (such as duke of Buckingham) or is received when the queen bestows a title on someone who has performed outstanding service to the country. The House of Lords plays no real part in the actual governing of Britain. It is the House of Commons and a Cabinet of about twenty ministers chosen from the House of Commons or the House of Lords by the prime minister who really govern.

The 1945 election was the first in which Margaret took an active part. She did all the usual things a young, inexperienced political volunteer does, from distributing literature to urging people to get out and vote. She even made some speeches, which, she confessed, "I quite enjoyed."

Although her choice, Quintin Hogg, retained his seat in the House of Commons, this election turned into a smashing victory for the Labour party. Britain's famed wartime leader, Conservative Winston Churchill, was defeated, and the number of Conservatives in Parliament slipped by 219 members. The Conservatives, now out of power, became the Opposition, the term used to describe the minority party in the House of Commons.

The war ended that same year, and many returning servicemen went back to the university. Even with the influx of male students, Margaret became the first woman ever elected president of the OUCA. Those same qualities which, years later, propelled her into the highest elected office in her country were obvious then. According to Maurice Chandler, secretary of the OUCA at the time, she was a "good organizer, extremely capable, intelligent, and sociable."

OUCA president was a golden position for a future politician. Leading Conservatives regularly gave OUCA-sponsored talks, and Margaret, as president, had to escort them around Oxford. In this way, she came to know many important Conservatives, some of whom became her close advisers as she moved up the political ladder.

Margaret wanted to give up chemistry and concentrate on politics. Like many other college students, she had to train for a profession in which she could earn enough money to support herself. Her father helped with her university expenses as much as he could. She worked at the local armed services canteen, and on vacation she taught mathematics and chemistry at the Grantham Central School for Boys.

Then the new Labour government increased the salaries of members of Parliament (MPs) to £1,000 (£ is the symbol for pound, an amount of English money). At that time, this meant that MPs were going to receive approximately $4,000. That was all the impetus Margaret needed. She was heard to say, "I *ought* to be an MP!"

At the end of four years at Oxford University, Margaret received a Bachelor of Science degree. She also holds a Master of Arts (M.A.) degree from Oxford. For the next four years, from 1947 to 1951, she worked for various companies as a research chemist, attempting to develop a special adhesive for British Xylonite Plastics, and for the famous food company J. Lyons, trying to find an emulsion that would preserve the foam in artificial ice cream. She worked briefly as personal assistant to the director of the Joint Iron Council.

During the day, while her mind concentrated on chemistry, her heart was in politics. While living in Colchester, an industrial town approximately sixty miles from London, she joined the Conservative Association. Politics became the focal point of her social life, as it had been at Oxford. Now she took a more active part, as she later explained it, by being a "potboiler, going around village halls keeping the audience warm until the candidate arrives."

In 1949 she got her first big political break. She was chosen to represent Oxford graduates at the annual Conservative Party Conference.

For Margaret, this conference at Llandudno, Wales, proved the first real step on her road to becoming prime minister. She was nominated to run (or "stand," as the English call it) for Parliament by the Dartford Conservative Committee. Dartford always votes for Labour; it is considered a "safe" seat, a sure win, for the Labour party. By running against a safe-seat candidate, even though there is little chance of being elected, a person can become known to his or her own party.

Someone told John Miller, chairman of the Dartford Conservative Committee that he knew of a possible Conservative candidate for the Dartford seat. Mr. Miller asked "his" name. Told the potential candidate was a woman, he frowned and replied, "That's most unsuitable." But once he met her, according to his wife, he became enthusiastic about her.

Margaret Phillimore, another committee member, remembers, "It was obvious to us that she had a marvelous brain. She was very poised, even as a twenty-three-year-old, but human and likable and good company."

There was a dinner in her honor to celebrate her nomination. By the time the meal ended, all public transportation from Llandudno to London had ceased for the evening. Margaret had to get to London. She needed to catch a train to Colchester so she could go to work the next morning.

The day—or night—was saved by Denis Thatcher, a former Royal Artillery officer. He offered to drive her to London.

Margaret was now a public figure, a candidate for Parliament, with her name and picture in the newspapers. At the same time, she led a private life, one of getting up early each morning to go to work to support herself (like thousands of other young women) and of a growing affection for Denis Thatcher.

After the Llandudno Conference in 1949, Margaret's life was never the same.

Margaret and Denis Thatcher leave Wesley's Chapel, London, after their wedding ceremony on December 13, 1951.

"I must get Denis some bacon."

3

"She rather pulled Denis out of a hat," claims Margaret Phillimore, so private was Denis and Margaret's friendship during the two and a half years before their engagement was announced.

According to Margaret Phillimore, "She was so occupied with politics and with her job that she didn't have time for a boyfriend." Or so it seemed to her friends.

At first glance, Denis and Margaret seem to have little in common. Denis loves sports, powerful cars, and fast driving. Margaret has no interest in sports, and driving fast scares her. He has no interest in music, the love of her life next to her job and her family. He likes to smoke; Margaret disapproves. But they both have a knowledge of chemistry, and they share an interest in politics, though Denis has no desire to be actively involved.

Denis inherited Atlas Preservatives, a paint and wallpaper company that had been founded by his grandfather. A Methodist, Denis drove a Jaguar, had his own apartment in London, was divorced, and was ten years older than Margaret.

In the 1950 election, Denis was there to cheer her on while she waged a vigorous campaign. Although Dartford is a large district, Margaret managed to meet all the campaign workers and earn their loyalty. Most of them have remained devoted to her ever since.

Although she has a reputation for being distant and hard to know, those who work with her usually become her fans.

During her campaign, she gave talks whenever she had the opportunity, and once in Bexley she spoke on women's rights.

"Don't be scared," she told her audience, "of the high-flown language of economists and cabinet ministers, but think of politics at our own household level." She then went on to speak of food supplies, housing shortages, and opportunities for children as three areas of concern homemakers shared with politicians.

When the election took place, Margaret, defeated as expected, surprised everyone by increasing the Tory (Conservative) vote by half, a minor miracle in a "safe" Labour district.

In Britain, general elections are held every five years unless the prime minister meets great opposition. After the 1950 election, the Labour prime minister, Clement Attlee, found himself with only a five-seat majority. It was obvious that his government could not continue for long.

Eighteen months later, a general election was held. Once more Margaret hoped to be elected to Parliament. Once more she was defeated. That night, however, was not a complete disappointment; Denis Thatcher surprised everyone by announcing that he and Margaret were going to get married.

Margaret and Denis chose December 13 for their wedding. Always the individualist, Margaret's bridal gown was not the traditional white lace and satin but velvet, in a shade of blue often called Tory blue. "It was deep winter and I wasn't going to be cold," she explains. Her hat, worn toward the back of her head, sported a large plume that followed the curve of her face.

Denis's influence on Margaret is enormous. He is a businessman and understands such things as finance and industry's problems. She consults him frequently. She appears more relaxed when he is there, and when a conference drags on until the early hours of the morning, he has been known to break it up by telling her it's time to go to bed. It is an extremely workable marriage.

After their honeymoon in Spain and Portugal, the Thatchers lived in Denis's small sixth-floor apartment in Swan Court, Flood Street. Every morning Denis left for work, and Margaret filled her days reading, attending lectures at the Council of Legal Education, and continuing her study of law, which she had begun shortly before her marriage.

Until now, she had always roomed where meals were provided. With a husband to feed, Margaret did the marketing and the cooking. To her surprise, she discovered she enjoyed visiting the shops and preparing the meals.

To this day, her cooking is restricted to plain dishes that taste good, look appetizing, require little preparation, and are liked by Denis. Even as prime minister, Margaret makes sure Denis has the food he likes. Once, during a briefing for a Cabinet meeting, she suddenly said, "I must get Denis some bacon." When asked why she didn't let one of the office girls get it, she answered, "No, they won't know what kind of bacon he likes."

She put on her hat, coat, and gloves, and walked to Shepherd Market. (Shepherd Market is a well-known section of London. It is a "village" of narrow streets, designed and built by Edward Shepherd in the eighteenth century.) Margaret bought the pound of bacon, returned to her office, and, sitting down, said, "Now, where were we?"

During her domestic years, Margaret's desire to be elected to Parliament never dimmed. Becoming pregnant did not stop her from preparing to pass her bar (law) exams and for a parliamentary career. Nineteen fifty-three was a memorable year. As Denis proudly tells it, "Bar intermediate in May, produced twins in August, and bar finals in December! I'd like to meet another woman who can equal that record."

The twins, Mark and Carol, were born prematurely on a day

that England won a major cricket match called the Ashes. Sports-loving Denis was out celebrating. No one could find him!

From the start, the twins have differed from each other in personality and interests. Mark takes after their father, Carol after their mother. Because Margaret's childhood was, by most standards, somewhat bleak, she determined that her children would have the advantages she had lacked. They took dancing lessons, learned to ride horseback, and went home with friends for meals.

The Thatchers had outgrown their living quarters. By renting the apartment next door and knocking a hole through the wall, they doubled the size. Margaret took over the decorating and, wearing large overalls, painted and wallpapered the rooms herself. This was her way of relaxing. Never satisfied with shoddy results, she did an excellent job. Eventually, the Thatchers purchased a house on Flood Street, directly across from Denis's original apartment.

The birth of the twins caused Margaret to postpone running for office again until they were old enough for school. This did not mean that she planned to stay home. With a nanny (full-time babysitter) to care for her children, Margaret was free to pursue her legal career.

Understanding taxes is an important part of government, so Margaret picked tax law as her specialization.

"I was really keenly interested in the financial side of politics, and so I went into the revenue side of law," she says.

But at 5:30 sharp, she rushed home to be with the twins, to feed them their supper and to spend time with them before tucking them into bed.

When the twins were six years old, Margaret decided to return to politics. In England, a person who wishes to be nominated to run for Parliament submits his or her name to the party's selection committee for the district he or she wishes to represent. It is not necessary to live in that district.

Margaret refused to be away from the twins for even one night, so she needed to find a district close to London. She finally decided on Beckenham in Kent. Much to her annoyance, she was turned down. The committee members told her she should stay home with her children.

She was more successful in submitting her name to the Finchley Conservative Association's Selection Committee. As John Tiplady said, "I know it may seem like hindsight, but when we interviewed the candidates, we asked ourselves, 'Is this a future prime minister?' Margaret clearly was and everyone thought so."

Denis, on his way home from a South African business trip, learned about his wife's selection when he picked up a London newspaper.

Finchley is considered a "safe" Conservative district, but Margaret didn't assume she would win. Up and down the area she campaigned, visiting schools, giving speeches, and impressing those she met with her amazing knowledge and memory. At a large meeting, she conducted an auction to raise money and correctly called out the names of a great number of people she had been introduced to just that evening. Everyone was astonished!

On October 8, 1959, five days before her thirty-fourth birthday, Margaret Thatcher was elected to Parliament. Twelve days later, she entered the House of Commons as a member of the majority party. Conservative Harold Macmillan was prime minister.

The sixty-eight-foot-long chamber of the House of Commons is divided into two sides, with bleachers of green leather facing each other. Members of the Opposition fill one side, the party in power the other. In the space between is the table of the clerk who records the happenings. Party leaders, junior ministers, and aides sit on the lower rows and are called "front-benchers." As a newcomer, Margaret joined the "back-benchers." At that time, the House of Commons had 630 members (it is up to approximately 650 now).

Strangely enough, there are seats for only 437 members. This was done deliberately. The House of Commons was bombed during

World War II. In planning the size of the new chamber, Prime Minister Winston Churchill stressed that "it should not be big enough to contain all its members without overcrowding." His reason: most debates would be held in a half-empty chamber, because not all members attend every day when the Commons is in session. Sir Winston believed that the house should be small enough for "the conversational style, the facility for quick, informal interruption . . . . there should be a sense of crowd and urgency."

A first speech is an ordeal faced by all new members. Margaret's lasted twenty-seven minutes, and the bill she introduced, called "Public Bodies (Admission of the Press to Meetings) Bill," was eventually passed. She received praise for her delivery. In fact, one comment foretold the future: "a speech of front-bench quality."

Margaret worked hard, involving herself in various controversial bills. Her speeches were always thoroughly researched. In the beginning years, she did it all herself, spending many hours in the House of Commons library. She usually stunned the Opposition by her vast knowledge of the subject being debated, and she loved to throw in statistics to prove her point.

In 1961, after two years as a back-bencher, she was rewarded. Lunching one day with her sister Muriel, Margaret received word that the prime minister wanted to see her. She hurried to No. 10 Downing Street. There Macmillan appointed her parliamentary secretary of the Ministry of Pensions and National Insurance.

Margaret had moved to the front bench.

Mrs. Thatcher is pictured with her six-year old twins, Carol and Mark, on September 11, 1959, a month before she was first elected to Parliament.

4

Margaret, now a junior minister, enjoyed the work she did in the Ministry of Pensions and National Insurance. She dealt with finance and welfare, two areas that interested her.

Her duties included defending the government's policies. In March she amazed the other members of Parliament by the statistics she threw at them in a forty-four-minute speech—everything from the cost of living in smoking and nonsmoking homes to comparative values of pensions for various years.

Once, in the middle of a speech, an aide handed her some newly released statistics. At that time, Margaret was a pretty, attractively dressed young woman in her thirties. Excitedly she exclaimed, "Gentlemen, I have the latest red-hot figure!" The House of Commons burst into laughter.

Although Margaret Thatcher was becoming well known for her parliamentary activities, she kept her home life private. Even today, the only people who really know her intimately are her husband and children, and they do not talk about her.

During this period, when her work load increased, the Thatchers were fortunate in having a wonderful nanny, Abbey, to look after the twins. Margaret never for a moment let them think they were unimportant to her. Motherhood meant a great deal to her, and she fussed and worried about her children.

Her own mother died in December 1960, and Margaret had a hard time getting over her death. Her father surprised everyone a few years later by remarrying.

Every year Denis and Margaret took the twins on vacation, usually to the beach. Once, when the twins were seven, Mark came down with chicken pox and the vacation had to be postponed. To make up for the twins' disappointment, the family went skiing in Switzerland at Christmas. They had such a good time that skiing for two weeks became an annual event.

This did not eliminate the summer vacation at the beach. They frequently chose to spend three weeks in August on the Isle of Wight. It was lots of fun for all four Thatchers. Margaret, relaxing away from Parliament, even designed costumes for a fancy-dress party.

At this time, things were not going well for Prime Minister Harold Macmillan (nicknamed "Super Mac") and the Conservative party. The economy slowed, unemployment rose, and members of the Cabinet differed with the prime minister and resigned. In October 1963, Macmillan himself resigned, and the next prime minister, Sir Alec Douglas-Home, did not have the support of the people.

When the Labour party won an election, Margaret had a hard fight to keep her seat in the House of Commons. She did, though, partly because of her activities for the people in her constituency. They wrote to her of their problems—everything from a son who couldn't find a job to the case of a neighbor, Gerald Brooke, arrested on spying charges by the KGB in Moscow in 1965. She took their troubles to heart and tried to help them, including stirring up such a fuss that Brooke was eventually released.

The Conservative party was without a leader, and the man Margaret backed, Edward Heath, got the position. Margaret has been called a lucky politician, and now came one of the times when she was considered fortunate. Back in 1964, few Conservative MPs were women. Margaret received more publicity than the men MPs, of which there were a far greater number and who were therefore not as newsworthy. She was pretty and photogenic as well. That plus her competence as a speaker, her thorough research of an issue, and her dedication to seeing a task through to the end brought her to the attention of the party leaders. Her rapid rise to power dates from "Ted" Heath's leadership.

They were friendly but not friends. It has been said Heath disliked two things above all else: women and people who disagreed with him. Margaret struck out on both counts. But Heath was smart and recognized her ability. He gave Margaret the job of front-bench spokesperson for the Opposition. She received a great deal of publicity, for this meant that she was supposed to challenge the Labour members of Parliament on their policies on such subjects as housing, transportation, and taxes. In 1966, Margaret's reputation as a speaker was firmly cemented by her response to a speech by Labourite John Diamond regarding a new kind of tax on employers.

During its delivery, she excitedly exclaimed, "This is sheer lunacy, absolute lunacy. I really think the chancellor [of the exchequer, or treasury] needs a woman in the treasury." This was a favorite joke between her and her secretary, Diana Powell. Margaret thought that a woman would not become prime minister in her lifetime and the highest post she could reach would be chancellor of the exchequer (the same as the secretary of the Treasury in the United States). Diana teased Margaret about becoming the first woman chancellor. Neither of them dreamed Margaret was destined to be prime minister.

The more active her parliamentary career, the less time Margaret had for home and family, yet her concern for her children's welfare was never relegated to the back of her mind.

Eating dinner with the twins became a rare event. The House of Commons convenes Monday through Thursday at 2:30 P.M., which leaves the mornings free for conferences, letters, speech writing, research, and, in Margaret's case, car-pooling children to school. The sessions usually last until 10:30 P.M. On Fridays, the members arrive for an 11:00 A.M. opening and finish up around 4:30 P.M.

Margaret continued to be associated with a legal firm (or "in chambers," as the English call it) until she was appointed junior minister by Macmillan. Her calendar, crowded beyond belief, left her very little free time. Often she had to ask her secretary to take her place in the car pool to collect the twins after school. And sometimes her secretary trailed after her to take dictation while Margaret sat under the hair dryer!

Although the twins were well cared for by Abbey, their longtime nanny, the Thatchers followed English custom by sending their children to boarding school. Eight-year-old Mark entered his boarding school in 1961, with Carol leaving for hers two years later. Mark went to school first because in England boys usually go to boarding school at a younger age than girls.

Events were making changes in Denis's life, too. In 1965 his family company was purchased by Castrol, and Castrol, in turn, was bought by Burmah Oil. Until this happened, the Thatchers had been well off financially although not really rich. With the change of ownership of these companies, Denis acquired holdings that made him quite wealthy. Thus Margaret's political future was assured. Campaigning for political office is expensive, and Margaret had the financial backing she needed to continue. She did not have to worry about household chores, because there was money for domestic help. This left her free to pursue her favorite job, being a member of Parliament.

In Britain, the leader of the Opposition appoints a "shadow Cabinet." The members of this Cabinet are to shadow, or keep track of, their equivalent in the real Cabinet. For example, in October 1967, Heath appointed Margaret shadow minister of power. Her job consisted of discovering everything that was happening at the Ministry of Power and challenging those things which she and the Conservatives did not like. Gas, coal, electricity, and nuclear energy were her concern.

Shadow minister of transportation and then shadow secretary of education and science were her next appointments. In this way, she gained knowledge of the inner workings of several departments, and these assignments became a training ground for her future as prime minister.

Then, in 1970, Margaret found herself secretary of state for education and science when the Conservatives won an election. Forty-five-year-old Margaret Thatcher now served in a Cabinet position, which placed her at the center of her country's government. Her only regret was that her father had not lived to see it happen. He died shortly before she took her place in the Cabinet.

Although the position does not sound like one of the most vital to the country, it actually stirred up heated feelings. England was in the process of restructuring its school system. Margaret's right, as secretary of education, to veto any proposed changes in a school organization handed her great power.

But Margaret faced a difficult situation made more difficult when the prime minister planned to cut government spending by about £300 million—at the time, about $720 million. Almost a third of the reduction came from the education budget. What could Margaret do to maintain an excellent standard of education? What could she eliminate? No matter what decision she reached, she was sure to anger some people.

As she saw it, her first duty was to provide the best possible education for the student. The solution she adopted proved to be one of the most unpopular moves in her career—up to and including the decisions she has reached as prime minister.

The previous Labour government had cut out free milk for older students; Margaret eliminated free milk for the lower grades. The idea, originally proposed in a Cabinet meeting, did not have Margaret's support in the beginning, but eventually she agreed.

She said, "I took the view that most parents are able to pay for milk for their children, and that the job of the government was to provide such things in education which they couldn't pay for, like new primary schools."

"Mrs. Thatcher, milk snatcher," was screamed at her.

For the first time in her career, she became the target of physical violence from a mob.

Margaret Thatcher was frequently in the news as she carried out one of the most difficult jobs of her career—secretary of state for education and science.

5

Margaret's popularity with students reached an all-time low when she tried to squeeze the expense of the education program into the government's budget in 1971. To do so, favorite measures of the students were cut.

"Mrs. Thatcher, milk snatcher," hurled at Margaret by demonstrators, did not seem as bad as some of the other names that she was called. In November 1971, a newspaper, the *Sun*, claimed that she was the "most unpopular woman in Britain." But worst of all were the times when she rose to speak in the House of Commons and members of the Opposition called out, "The minister of lost opportunity," "Mrs. Scrooge with a painted face," and, perhaps worst of all, "Ditch the bitch!"

All this unpleasantness was not caused solely by the stopping of the free milk program. Margaret, surrounded by a variety of problems, fought to do what she considered best for her country and its students. University students never agreed with her.

Obviously, with the education budget reduced by millions, cuts in funding had to be made in other ways than just free milk. So Margaret took a close look at student unions. Many universities required students to be members, and the students backed causes that had nothing to do with education. For example, helping citizens of African countries fight for freedom and supporting striking dock workers were not, in Margaret's opinion, legitimate purposes for student union dues. Many of these students had obtained government grants to pay for their university expenses, which included student union dues. Margaret maintained that taxpayers' money should not be spent to support such issues.

She recommended that the universities administer these monies, not the students. This set off violent protests throughout Britain.

Bad experiences followed Margaret wherever she went. Students would not come forward to receive awards from her; some did not show up to eat lunch when she was guest of honor; others walked out while she was speaking; and in London during her talk, students gathered outside to scream, "If you hate Thatcher, clap your hands!"

In Liverpool, the noise was so great no one could hear what she said, and the air in the auditorium was filled with flying objects, mostly paper airplanes. To her friend Guinevere Tilney, Margaret confessed it had been a rowdy meeting. She showed Guinevere a large bruise where she had been struck in the chest by a stone.

When Guinevere asked what she had done when it hit her, Margaret answered, "I went on speaking. What else could I do?"

Through all this, she remained outwardly calm, showing no emotion, and gaining for herself a reputation of being unfeeling and cold. She has never been able to shake this picture of herself.

Once, at a dinner party, just as everyone fell silent, a voice asked, "Is there any truth in the rumor that Mrs. Thatcher is a woman?"

Margaret, sitting a few seats away, pretended not to hear.

Denis worried about her and suggested she consider giving up politics. The twins suffered, especially Carol, who was attending the University of London during this period. Other students acted as though she were responsible for her mother's actions. She was shunned, ignored when not the butt of nasty remarks, and made thoroughly miserable.

In February 1974, Prime Minister Heath decided to hold a general election. The Conservatives found the going rough. The Amalgamated Union of Engineering called a series of one-day strikes that closed factories, shipyards, newspapers, and some power plants. Britain suffered a shortage of electricity. Then came the coal miners' strike. And to top it off, the Arabs issued an oil embargo after the Yom Kippur War of 1973 in an attempt to keep Western nations from aiding Israel.

Denis Thatcher probably sighed in relief that Margaret's forty months as secretary of state for education and science were over when Labour won the election. Although Harold Wilson's Labour party had won by only four seats in the House of Commons, he returned to No. 10 Downing Street as prime minister.

Margaret had proved herself under fire. Perhaps Conservative party leader Heath, who had just been voted out as prime minister, agreed with one of her most quoted remarks: "If you want something said, ask a man. If you want something done, ask a woman." Heath immediately handed her another difficult job. He appointed her shadow minister of the environment.

In this position, Margaret was faced with a conflict of ideas. As a deeply committed Tory, strongly opposed to government interference in private enterprise, she found herself forced to support government-controlled mortgage rates and government aid to housing. These were part of the Conservative party policy. If she resigned and returned to the back bench in the House of Commons, she would probably never again be appointed to the Cabinet—shadow or the real thing.

Convinced that her brand of Conservatism was necessary to lead England away from the Labour party's policy of government taking over industry, she determined to stick it out. But Margaret Thatcher was beginning to doubt her party's leadership.

A real crisis loomed for the Conservative party as Labour won another general election in October, the second held in 1974. While campaigning, Conservatives were told time and time again, "We'd vote for you except for Heath." Back-benchers appeared ready to revolt against Ted Heath's leadership.

Just at this moment, Heath appointed Margaret to be second Opposition spokesperson in the House of Commons on treasury affairs. She paid special attention to finance bills and those on public spending proposed by the now-in-power Labour government.

For Heath, it proved a fatal appointment. Margaret quickly did an excellent job of pointing out the flaws in Labour's Finance Bill. Her speeches, full of scorn for the new Labour bill, brought cheers from Conservative back-benchers. For the first time, they began to wonder if it were possible to have a woman party leader.

Ted Heath did not want to resign. He not only enjoyed being party leader, he believed himself best qualified for the job. But he had no choice. When the Conservatives are out of power (or "in opposition"), an election for party leader is held every year.

One by one, others who might have been elected to replace Heath dropped out. Although just a short time before Margaret had told a television audience that, "It will be years before a woman either leads the party or becomes prime minister," she began to wonder if that might be changed. Why couldn't she run for party leader?

Her decision was made, it is claimed, without consulting anyone, not even Denis (though that seems hard to believe). As always, she worried how this would affect her children. At her mother's suggestion, Carol was studying law at the University of London. When Mark turned down a chance to go to Oxford University, Margaret sadly commented, "For my father, unthinkable. For me, a dream. For my son, a refusal. All in three generations."

Mark went to work for a firm of accountants, apparently following his father's lead. His main interest, however, was cars, and he really wanted to devote himself to automobiles.

Yet, concerned as she was about the changes in her family's lives if she became party leader, there was no one else who had, she explained, "the thoughts and ideas I had, and it seemed to be absolutely vital for the country that I stood" (ran).

Those who backed her included Airey Neave, a World War II hero, whose exploits were the kind that inspire television's wildest adventure stories. The first Allied officer to escape from Colditz, a German prisoner-of-war camp thought to be impossible to break out of, he returned to Germany to organize a way other escaping POWs could reach safety. After the war, he entered politics. A promising start as a junior minister was cut short by a heart attack which sent him to the back bench.

Neave was highly respected. He suggested to some Conservative members of the House of Commons that they switch to backing Margaret, and they did. This represented an important step in gathering supporters for Margaret. Neave was a wonderful organizer, and he took over managing her campaign. The three candidates for party leader were Ted Heath, Margaret Thatcher, and Hugh Fraser, who ran primarily as an option for those who did not want either Heath or a woman!

By election day, February 4, 1975, very few believed Margaret had a chance of winning. This was not, of course, a general election; it was an election within the Conservative party by members of the House of Commons. Margaret waited in Neave's small office while Conservative members filed into Parliament's Committee Room 14 to vote. To win on the first ballot, a candidate needed 139 votes; otherwise, a second ballot was necessary.

At 4:00 that afternoon, the results were announced: Margaret had received 130 votes, Mr. Heath 119, and Mr. Fraser 16; 11 MPs had abstained from voting. When Margaret heard the figures, she kissed her friend Nigel Fisher on both cheeks and exclaimed, "Isn't it exciting, Nigel? Isn't it exciting?"

A week of feverish activity followed as her supporters tried to sway MPs to support Margaret. Voting fell on the same day—February 11—that Carol had to take one of two remaining exams to pass the bar and become a solicitor (lawyer).

Carol and her mother sat in the kitchen that morning, each tense at the important event in her life scheduled to occur that day.

Finally Margaret said, "Good luck, darling. You can't be as nervous as I am!"

As Carol's exam ended, one of the proctors asked her if she had heard the results of the Conservative party election. He was the one to tell her that her mother was the new party leader. The final count gave 146 votes to Margaret.

Now, for the first time, a woman not only led a party but also stood a chance of becoming prime minister. It was, indeed, an exciting moment!

President Gerald Ford and Margaret Thatcher enjoyed a visit on September 18, 1975, when she became the first Opposition party leader to be invited to the White House.

6

As leader of the Opposition, Margaret faced a variety of questions:
Would the delegates to the annual Conservative party conference
back her the way the MPs had? Would voters remember the excellent job she had done as shadow secretary of the environment and
spokesperson on treasury affairs instead of her unpopularity during
the free-milk crisis? Would they vote for Conservative candidates
knowing if that party won an election, a woman would hold the most
powerful position in the country, that of prime minister?

What about the people in the north of England and in Scotland?
They scarcely knew her; would they accept her? And what about
the areas in which she was inexperienced, such as foreign affairs?
Would that influence voters?

These were political problems. On a personal level, she had to
reach decisions as well.

Although her appearance had always been of great importance
to her, the press had often pointed out that her way of dressing was
not stylish. With every moment of her day recorded by the media,
now seemed a perfect time to change her image.

She turned to her friend Guinevere Tilney to help her to become
more fashionable. They experimented with various styles of dress,

makeup experts, and hairdressers, although years before Margaret had begun touching up the gray in her hair.

Gordon Reece, former TV producer and at that time director of publicity for the Conservative party, worried about her reputation for being cold and aloof. Thinking that a warmer-sounding voice would help, he told her to stand closer to the microphone. Instead of warm, her voice came across as sexy! One newspaper decided she must have a sore throat!

"I've never been so insulted in my life!" Margaret laughed.

Her most immediate political job was appointing members of her shadow cabinet. In this Airey Neave helped; he became shadow minister of Northern Ireland.

She made her own appointments, however, firing almost all who had been Heath supporters. Surprisingly, she kept two, because she felt they were the best people for the job: Sir Geoffrey Howe as chief opposition spokesman for treasury and Sir Ian Gilmour for home affairs.

She had to attend functions and give talks that had been scheduled for Ted Heath. She had always written her own; now her crowded calendar left little time for speech writing.

Although they had never met, she decided to give a chance to a former Heath speech writer, Ronnie Miller. A playwright, Ronnie sat in a darkened theater during the rehearsal of a play and wrote his first speech for Margaret. It ended with a quote from Abraham Lincoln, part of which reads: "You cannot bring about prosperity by discouraging thrift. You cannot strengthen the weak by weakening the strong. You cannot help the poor by destroying the rich."

After Ronnie finished reading the speech to Margaret, she silently reached into her purse and took a yellowing paper from her wallet. Unfolding it, she handed it to Ronnie. Written on it was the same Lincoln quote.

"I never go anywhere without it," she said.

From that moment on, Ronnie joined her group of trusted helpers.

Margaret's days centered on working for a Conservative victory in the next election. To do so, she had to prove to voters she was capable of leading the country.

This involved more travel than she had ever done. First came trips to the north of England and Scotland where she made a big hit. Then to European countries to learn more about foreign affairs: Luxembourg, France, Germany, and Rumania. Next came North America with visits to Canada and the United States.

Her greatest success came on her second visit to the United States in 1975. It had been a policy for the president never to receive the leader of an opposition party. (France's François Mitterrand had been turned down for that reason.) President Gerald Ford, ignoring the custom of meeting only with heads of state, invited Margaret into the Oval Office. Obviously, Margaret Thatcher had arrived on the international scene!

In Chicago, she was asked if she preferred being called "Mrs." or "Ms."

"I am not sure I fully understand the significance of your question. I am just Margaret Thatcher. You must take me as I am," she answered.

By the time of the annual conference, Margaret had convinced the delegates she made a good leader. They cheered and cheered when she told them her vision of the future.

"A man's right to work as he will. To spend what he earns. To own property. To have the state as servant and not as master. These are the British inheritance."

Invitations from nations around the world continued to pour in. Everyone wanted to meet the woman who might become Britain's prime minister. When she headed for the Far East, Carol went along. Carol needed time away from England, away from the publicity she received as a party leader's daughter. She planned to visit friends in Australia.

She and Margaret said good-bye in Hong Kong, believing they would be separated only six months. But Carol did not move back to England until five years later.

In the spring, a year and a half after Margaret stepped into history by being elected the first woman leader of a political party in England, an unexpected event took her closer to becoming prime minister. The Labour prime minister, Harold Wilson, announced his resignation. No one knows exactly why. Labour had a majority of only one seat in Parliament. Some claim he felt the Conservatives would win in the next election and he did not want to be beaten. Some said his wife detested his being prime minister.

The Labour members chose James Callaghan to succeed Mr. Wilson. This did not please Margaret, who had hoped for a general election.

Elections are held in England every five years unless members of the House of Commons vote they have "no confidence" in the party in power. Then Parliament is dissolved, campaigns are waged, a general election is held, and it is up to the people to decide if they agree. If they do, the other party takes over with its leader filling the job of prime minister. If not, the party in power continues.

General elections may be held at other times, too. The prime minister usually calls for one when he or she feels sure the party in power is popular and will win. It is a way of extending the prime minister's five years into a longer period.

Margaret did not like Callaghan. He always spoke to her in a very condescending way. Once he jeered, "Now, now, little lady, you don't want to believe all those things you read in newspapers about crisis and upheavals and the end of civilization as we know it. Dearie me, not at all!"

Margaret tried to get the House of Commons to vote "no

confidence" in Mr. Callaghan's government, but the MPs refused to go along with her.

Margaret's work load during this period was even greater than it had been. When she arrived home from a night session of the Commons, she had to prepare for the next day and read all the paperwork that had gathered during the hours she had been in the House. It was extremely important that she attend, for as leader of the Opposition, she had to know exactly what was being said in the debates about government policies.

Margaret quickly discovered her own home suffered. "The house is not as perfect as I would like because I haven't time to make it so," she said.

Even with all the pressures, Margaret never forgot a birthday or a thoughtful gesture. Once, in 1977, a very dear friend and fellow Conservative MP, Fergus Montgomery, was accused of shoplifting. Margaret showed her faith by spending an afternoon deep in conversation with him as they walked up and down the corridors of the houses of Parliament. She made sure they were seen together, and when he was acquitted, she amazed everyone by kissing him in the Members' Bar—a place she rarely went.

Margaret has never been afraid to tackle an unpopular subject. "We are not in politics to ignore people's worries," she declared. "We are in politics to deal with them."

Although England was experiencing race riots after an enormous influx of Asians, West Indians, Africans, Pakistanis, and others, immigration was a taboo subject to politicians. Sensing a rising tide of racial problems, most MPs sidestepped the issue.

Not Margaret! As these peoples brought with them cultures that differed greatly from Britain's, Margaret feared it would become impossible to preserve the British character. She said that the moment a minority becomes a big one, people get frightened and fearful of losing their jobs.

"Every country can take some small minorities and in many

ways they add to the richness and variety of this country," she stated. But immigration appeared out of control, and she recommended the government "hold out the clear prospect of an end of immigration."

Her views caused an uproar. She was accused of inciting race riots. However, her views proved to be popular. An election, held to fill a vacancy that had occurred by the death of MP Minnie Miller, resulted in an overwhelming Conservative victory and demonstrated that many Britons agreed with her.

Under Callaghan, the Labour party did not have an easy time. Debates on important issues in the House of Commons solved nothing. A proposed change in the governing of Scotland and Wales remained unresolved. Strikers who shut schools and hospitals were joined by garbage collectors, underground (subway) operators, and even grave diggers.

On March 28, 1979, Margaret Thatcher raised the issue of a no-confidence vote. A heated debate lasted for seven hours. By 10:00 P.M., the excitement and noise were so great that the Speaker could not get a vocal count. He sent no-confidence voters to the right-hand lobby, those against to the left. The Conservatives carried the no-confidence vote, but just barely: 311 to 310!

Now the big question: would the voters give the Conservatives a victory in the general election, making Margaret Thatcher Great Britain's first woman prime minister?

Margaret Thatcher and her husband arrive at No. 10 Downing Street on May 4, 1979, the day after she became the first woman to be elected prime minister.

7

Two days after the historic no-confidence victory, an elated Margaret visited her constituency of Finchley. There, a thirty-minute drive from the houses of Parliament, she opened a children's fair and chatted with local Conservatives about the coming election.

That afternoon, a little before three o'clock, Airey Neave walked from his office in the Commons to his car in the new parking facility. He opened the door and climbed in.

A remote control bomb, attached to the undercarriage of his car, detonated. The resulting explosion was heard by Margaret's staff and sent a column of smoke into the air alongside the Big Ben Tower.

Neave was pulled from the wreckage and rushed to a hospital. A war hero, decorated for bravery not only by his own country but by others as well, he died on the operating table, a victim of an Irish terrorist's bomb.

Margaret was devastated. He had been one of her earliest supporters, and she had relied heavily on his advice. Added to her grief was the knowledge that she had appointed him shadow minister for Northern Ireland, was expected to confirm his appointment to the same post in her new Cabinet, and therefore was indirectly responsible for his death. The awesome responsibility she had assumed had been vividly demonstrated.

Shortly after that, Carol returned from Australia to help her mother, who had thrown herself into the grueling pace of a political campaign. For four weeks Margaret was up at dawn and rarely asleep before 2:00 or 3:00 the next morning. She visited factories and farms and schools and shops and everything in between. Her picture was taken with workers, with shoppers, and with animals.

At the end of a whirlwind day, her campaign workers went back to the Thatchers', where Margaret, the perfect hostess, gave first place to worrying if her guests had enough food and drink, and campaign strategy took second place.

One invitation she turned down was to debate the current prime minister, Mr. Callaghan, on television. She wanted the election to be decided on issues and policies, not personalities. "We should stick to that approach," she said. "We are not electing a president. We are choosing a government."

By that, she was referring to the differences in the way the president of the United States and the prime minister of Great Britain chose their Cabinet members. In the United States, Cabinet members are appointed by the president and confirmed by the Senate.

The Conservative manifesto (in the United States, the party platform) declared: "This election is about the future of Britain—a great country which seems to have lost its way." Margaret's main objective was to stop the "slither and slide to a socialist state."

Her promises included cutting income taxes, trimming government spending except for defense, turning state-owned industries back into private companies, and tackling the all-powerful labor unions, which, with their demands, had held the Labour government hostage. She declared that the majority of union workers were responsible people but there were a "few thousand wreckers . . . we have to mobilize the rest of the members against."

She also maintained, "I intend to try not to make any promises which I might not be able to deliver."

May 3, the Thursday of the election, dawned bitterly cold. For the second day, an unseasonal blizzard blanketed the western and northern parts of the country. As much as five inches of snow fell in some places.

If Margaret did not win a majority of votes in Finchley she would no longer be a member of Parliament and leader of the Conservative party. If the Conservatives won, she could become prime minister. She spent much of the day at home and then, like any politician, went to her constituency, Finchley. Once the votes in Finchley had been counted and she was sure of her victory, Margaret and her family drove to the Conservative party central office.

She remained there until 5:00 A.M. on Friday, when partial results showed the Conservatives with a forty-four-seat majority in the House of Commons. Even at that hour, the Thatcher home was surrounded by flag-waving, cheering crowds. Margaret herself did not go to bed at all.

Did this mean she, as leader of the majority party, was now automatically prime minister?

No. There cannot be two prime ministers at the same time. James Callaghan had not resigned. Officially he was prime minister until he handed his resignation to the queen. His successor would not take office until Queen Elizabeth summoned her to Buckingham Palace and asked if she could form a government. When told yes, the queen would then instruct her to do so.

The role of the queen in English government is unique. She is head of the state; indeed, it is called "Her Majesty's government." Although her power is limited, she still performs certain important acts of government, such as summoning and dissolving Parliament, giving royal assent to parliamentary bills, and appointing ministers of state, including the prime minister.

Kept fully informed, Queen Elizabeth knows more about what

is happening than anyone other than the prime minister. Whoever is prime minister confers with her once a week; she represents a continuity of governing and possesses a memory of past events to call upon which current politicians lack.

It wasn't until 2:45 P.M. on May 4, 1979, when the minimum (318) seats necessary for a majority in the House of Commons had been counted, that Margaret announced her victory and then sat down to wait the phone call from the palace.

In her book *Margaret Thatcher, Wife-Mother-Politician*, British author Penny Junor writes that after Margaret had spoken to the queen's representative at the palace, Mark put his arm around his mother and said proudly, "Prime Minister."

"Not yet," Margaret corrected.

"The car may break down," Denis contributed, referring to the ride to the palace.

"In that case," Margaret responded, "I shall walk!"

While Denis waited downstairs with palace aides, Margaret's audience with the queen lasted forty-five minutes. At the end of the audience, Margaret was the first woman prime minister of Great Britain.

The relationship between Margaret and the queen has caused speculation. Some say they get along very well. Every so often, a rumor starts that Margaret's manner irritates Queen Elizabeth. No one outside their immediate families really knows.

In the United States, two months elapse between the election and the inauguration of the new president, who then moves into the White House. In contrast, in Britain there is no waiting period between being elected, being appointed by the queen, and taking possession of No. 10 Downing Street.

Mr. Callaghan's aides were moving his things out the back door as Margaret Thatcher's were being carried in the front! The Thatchers went directly from Buckingham Palace to No. 10. The street was jammed with people. Standing on the steps, Margaret quoted from St. Francis of Assisi: "Where there is discord, may we bring harmony; where there is error, may we bring truth; where there is doubt, may we bring faith; and where there is despair, may we bring hope."

She then had a brief message, "To all the British people," which ended, "And, finally, one last thing; in the words of Airey Neave, whom we had hoped to bring here with us, 'Now there is work to be done.'"

The new prime minister soon made the acquaintance of a permanent resident of No. 10, a black-and-white tomcat named Wilberforce. He strayed into the official residence on Downing Street in 1973 and became a friend to four prime ministers. Often seen resting on the front doorstep, he received lots of fan letters. Mrs. Thatcher and Wilberforce always spoke to each other when they passed in the halls. Wilberforce died in his sleep in May 1988, fifteen years after moving into No. 10.

Margaret Thatcher set about her two most immediate projects: selecting her Cabinet and working on the queen's speech.

Cabinet ministers must be members of either the House of Commons or the House of Lords. From the House of Lords came Lord Carrington as foreign secretary. Conservative members of the House of Commons who filled important posts were Sir Geoffrey Howe as chancellor of the exchequer, Francis Pym as defense minister, and William Whitelaw as deputy prime minister.

The introduction of the new prime minister's official policies takes place when, in a colorful ceremony, the queen addresses both houses at the state opening of Parliament. This was to take place twelve days after the election.

Queen Elizabeth, dressed in robe and crown like a medieval monarch, rides to Parliament in a coach pulled by horses. Members of the Commons wait for the appearance of the "Black Rod," an honorary title which carries as its main task notifying the prime minister and others in the Commons that it is time to go to the House of Lords to hear the queen's speech.

The queen never expresses her own thoughts or ideas on political matters. What Queen Elizabeth said had been carefully planned by Mrs. Thatcher and her policy advisers. It was the first time the nation learned exactly how Margaret Thatcher hoped to implement her campaign promises.

As was expected, the moment the queen left, it was back to business as usual, with Labour leaders attacking the prime minister's plans.

This was a taste of what a prime minister has to face regularly. One afternoon every week is question time. The "PM" must answer questions thrown at her by members of the Commons. (It is as if the president of the United States appeared in the House of Representatives and personally answered questions about his policies.) At this first conference, Margaret Thatcher displayed logical thinking in her answers.

Mrs. Thatcher aimed at completely reversing the trend toward government control of industries, housing, education, and health care that had taken place since World War II. She strongly believes that private enterprise is best for the British people.

A great howl followed the announcement of the first budget with its massive cuts and reduction of taxes. The going was exceedingly rough, with members of her own party—indeed, her own Cabinet—openly criticizing her.

But Margaret Thatcher had more on her mind than the budget. As prime minister, she must go to a meeting of the European Economic Council (EEC or Common Market). The Common Market consists of twelve nations that work together to increase European economic integration. In the beginning, this meant eliminating trade restrictions between the nations and controlling prices of certain products; from that has grown the European Community, and a desire to turn Europe into one country with one currency and one police force.

At the meeting in Strasbourg, France, she immediately demanded that Britain's monetary contribution be cut. This was her first appearance at a foreign meeting; she impressed the other delegates by her knowledge of the subject.

The many problems she faced included racial conflict in Rhodesia, the continual time bomb of Ireland, the fierce battle with powerful labor unions, inflation, and an alarming increase in unemployment.

As prime minister, Mrs. Thatcher cannot focus on one problem until it is solved and then go on to the next. Events take place simultaneously, both in her public life and private.

When, in 1980, Irish terrorists blew up the yacht on which the queen's seventy-nine-year old cousin Lord Louis Mountbatten was sailing, Margaret's concern for her children's safety became almost overwhelming. "This is serious," she told them, and she instructed them to follow police procedure, such as looking under their cars before climbing in.

Then, in 1982, Margaret experienced a personal event that tested her strength of character.

Her son, Mark, always interested in racing cars, participated in a Paris-to-Dakar (Africa) race. He and his co-driver, a very glamorous French girl, were missing in the Sahara, the large trackless desert. Soon reports came that they had been located, which sent everyone's hopes soaring, only to be followed by word that they had not been found.

The prime minister carried on with her work. Arriving to address a luncheon meeting, someone called out, "Any news?"

As she answered, "I'm sorry, there is no news," for the first time in her public life tears overflowed her eyes and rolled down her cheeks.

The prime minister had shown the world she had a very human side.

The prime minister and other dignitaries watch the Armed Forces salute to the Falkland Islands Task Force, October 12, 1982.

8

The days passed, and still no word that Mark and his companion were safe. Denis could stand the waiting no longer. Accepting an offer from a friend, he flew in a private plane to Africa to join in the search.

This was not the first time Mark had worried his parents with his driving escapades and his knack for making headlines. In 1980, he had agreed to act as a model for a Japanese textile company in exchange for their sponsoring him in a race. The Labour MPs from the cloth manufacturing areas were outraged. Then an Englishman offered to take over the sponsorship; unfortunately, he published a sex magazine, and another storm broke around Mark! Finally, Mark made a deal with a British racing team.

His narrow escapes included being pulled from a fiery crash, smashing through a barrier at high speed, having a violent accident two months later on a trial run for a race in Germany, and now being lost in the Sahara.

Six days later, Mark and his companion showed up. His mother, grateful but furious, is supposed to have lectured him on disappearing in the desert with a beautiful girl! The prime minister was also unhappy about the expense to the Algerian government as their soldiers had searched for him. (Ten months later, during a car rally, Mark was lost for eight hours on the Mexican desert!)

Later that year, 1982, Margaret Thatcher faced the hardest decision of her life: should Britain go to war?

Eight thousand miles away, a group of islands, the Falklands, lie about 300 miles from Argentina and approximately 700 miles from Antarctica. Over 200 of them break the surface of the South Atlantic; only 2 are large enough for towns. In the days of sailing ships, these strategically placed islands offered the closest shipyards for vessels damaged by the hurricane winds and wild seas around Cape Horn. They were also important to the whaling industry. With the building of the Panama Canal, their importance faded.

In the second half of the twentieth century, they are once more becoming valuable. In recent decades, the belief that oil, gold, and minerals exist in Antarctica has stirred great interest. The waters abound with krill, tiny crustaceans many people hope will provide cheap food for Third World nations. Many countries, including Britain, have established research stations there. The British Antarctic Territory is a dependency of the Falkland Islands, the British possession that is closest to Antarctica.

Today, 1,800 English-speaking people live on the Falklands. The earliest settlers were Spanish gauchos (who long ago left) and Scottish shepherds. Now owned by Britain, the islands have been the possession of France and Spain as well. France backed out by ceding her claims to Spain. At one time, England and Spain almost went to war over them. In 1771 Spain yielded her rights in them to Britain, but it wasn't until 1833 that the dispute with the "Republic of Buenos Aires" (the future Argentina) ended. Argentina has had her eye on them for many years.

In 1982 Argentina was in a state of upheaval. The junta (governing body) had deposed the president and appointed General Leopoldo Galtieri to head the country. He was not liked. His economic reform program brought thousands of rioting protesters into the streets. He hit upon the conquest of the Falklands as a means of securing much-needed popularity. Argentina, having agitated for them for twenty years, broke off peaceful negotiations with Britain. Suddenly the control of these islands gained crisis proportions.

Working in her office in the House of Commons around 7 P.M. on March 31, Margaret received word that the Argentine fleet had set sail and might be heading for the Falklands. Sir Henry Leach, the first sea lord, advised that it was possible for a task force to be ready to leave for the islands by April 5. First sea lord is the title of the man who heads the admiralty or naval affairs.

Margaret Thatcher notified President Reagan. U.S. military authorities responded that if Argentina invaded, it would be impossible for Britain to retake the islands. According to them, British lines of communication would be too long and air cover insufficient.

The prime minister did not want to fight. She was sick at the thought of war. She immediately tried to reopen negotiations with Argentina by asking President Reagan to send his secretary of state, Alexander Haig, to talk to them. Nothing came of General Haig's many flights between London and Buenos Aires. The secretary general of the United Nations, Javier Perez de Cuellar, joined in the commuting between the two cities but to no avail. Even so, no one in Britain really believed fighting would become necessary.

On April 2, Argentina invaded the islands. Mrs. Thatcher's future depended on the outcome of what happened on those barren, faraway islands. If Britain were unsuccessful, she would probably have to resign as prime minister, and her political career might be over. She gave no consideration to her own future, however, but took the action she believed right. Later on, she expressed her beliefs to writer John Newhouse. "You really cannot have people marching into other people's territory and staying there and winning the territory as a result of force. You cannot."

All the countries of the North Atlantic Treaty Organization (NATO) remained firmly behind Britain. The United States helped Britain, but how much and in what way continues to be a secret.

By the end of April, British ships arrived in the midst of winter storms. Even before the soldiers landed on the bleak islands came the distressing news of the sinking of the Argentine cruiser *General Belgrano*. Three hundred sixty-eight men were lost. After the war, when the prime minister was attacked by the Labour party for the decision to sink it, she expressed bitterness at their criticism. The *Belgrano* had been trailing two British aircraft carriers and might at any moment (as they got closer to the Falklands) attempt to sink them. Their safety plus that of the many troop transport ships rested on her shoulders.

It was later claimed that the *Belgrano* had changed course and appeared to be heading for its home port when it was sunk. Mrs. Thatcher may not have known this, however.

On May 19, 2,400 marines and paratroopers landed, and fighting began. Soon came reports of losses in both men and equipment. These were days of anguish for Mrs. Thatcher. Convinced her action was right, she shared the agony of the mothers, wives, and children whose men were being exposed to enemy fire. George Gale of the *Daily Express* reported her saying, "In a way, the Falklands became my life, it became my bloodstream."

When Mark had been missing in the Sahara, the queen, showing her concern, telephoned. Now it was the prime minister's turn to express her concern, because the queen's son, Prince Andrew, a helicopter pilot, was flying missions from the aircraft carrier *Invincible*. Finally June 14 dawned to reveal Argentine soldiers fleeing toward Stanley, the islands' capital. A white flag was soon spotted. By 9:00 A.M. the next day, the Argentine commander had surrendered. Major-General Moore issued a statement: "The Falkland Islands are once more under the government desired by their inhabitants. God save the queen!"

The invasion had been as important to the future of General Galtieri as for the prime minister. The humiliating defeat of his army forced him to resign three days later.

When Margaret Thatcher heard of the surrender, she eloquently expressed her feelings in just one word, "Rejoice!"

The prime minister now had to face the accusations of her opponents over the Falklands war. It was said that she misjudged the intentions of the Argentineans and must accept full responsibility for the war.

A commission was appointed. Six months later, it declared that she was in no way responsible. British intelligence had failed to notify her so she could take action prior to the invasion. British intelligence had, in fact, been taken by surprise.

With the Falklands war behind her, Mrs. Thatcher decided in July 1982 to correct a physical problem. Like many others who stand a great deal, she had trouble with her legs. On August 23 she underwent surgery for a circulatory problem. Denis called for her that evening; some say she refused to stay in the hospital overnight for fear of appearing a weak woman. Impressed, her doctor said, "She simply won't allow herself to be ill."

A month after her operation, she took off on an exhausting two-week journey to the Far East. After a stay in Japan, she became the first British prime minister to visit China. There, outside the Great Wall, she tripped and fell. Immediately jumping to her feet, she assured everyone she had not been hurt.

The visit to China was important because of the discussions held there about the status of Hong Kong, the next stop on her trip. An island at the mouth of the Pearl River, Hong Kong was ceded to Britain in 1841, and nineteen years later Stonecutters' Island and Kowloon became British as well.

In 1898 a ninety-nine-year lease with China turned over parts of the mainland, known as the New Territories, to Britain. The end of the lease is fast approaching; in 1997 the New Territories will be returned to China. But what about Hong Kong? China wants it, too. The population of over five million includes different nationalities, many of them American and British. Margaret Thatcher was concerned about what will happen to those living under the Chinese Communist government. It took two more years before an agreement was reached.

A year of stress, 1982 required historic decisions as well as personal inner strength. Shortly after the end of that year, Mrs. Thatcher, her emotions clearly showing on her face and accompanied by Denis, paid a surprise visit to the Falklands. Two hundred and fifty-five British subjects had died. "I felt every one," Margaret Thatcher said. Tears fell from her eyes at the War Graves Commission Cemetery. She received a heroine's welcome.

Now she faced another problem that involved both her private and public lives. In May 1983, four years of her five-year term would be over. All prime ministers try to pick a time when their popularity is high to hold a general election. Should Mrs. Thatcher wait until 1984 to schedule one? What unexpected event, what scandal might cause voters to turn against her? Already the press was speculating when the election would take place.

Mrs. Thatcher had to ask herself: Were the people of Britain still behind her?

The prime minister and her husband paid a surprise visit to the Falklands seven months after the end of the brief war. Here they are welcomed by General Commissioner Sir Rex Hunt and Lady Hunt.

*"There's far more understanding
and good sense in people than
some politicians give them
credit for."*

9

As winter progressed into spring, the speculation about a general election turned into demands for one. The Conservatives, fearful of an unknown future, were afraid to wait until Mrs. Thatcher's term in office ran out in 1984. They wanted her to ride the popularity winds that the Falkland war had created. The successful outcome of the fighting had united Britain and given a feeling of national pride that had been lacking since World War II.

The opposing parties were just as anxious, believing that criticism of the Falkland affair, a series of workers' strikes, and the high unemployment rate formed a winning combination for them.

The uncertainty of the outcome of the election was bad for the economy. For one thing, foreign investors delayed in deciding whether to place money in Britain until they knew which side won. In May 1983, Mrs. Thatcher announced that a general election was scheduled for June 9.

The campaign was nasty—perhaps nastier than usual—especially when the deputy leader of the Labour party, referring to the Falklands, claimed that the prime minister gloried in slaughter and wrapped herself in the flag. People, regardless of political affiliation, were stunned by his vicious attack. It probably lost many votes for the Labour candidates.

Knowing the Labour party would emphasize unemployment, Mrs. Thatcher, with her usual directness, confronted the problem in her first campaign talk. She pointed out that every Labour government had promised to reduce unemployment and had instead increased it. She could not deny, of course, that many were without jobs, but Britain was not alone in this. Everyone had thought that, with the advent of new technologies, more jobs would exist. They did later on, but during the 1970s and early 1980s, all of Western Europe suffered from jobs disappearing rather than being created. Even such a prosperous country as West Germany had the same problem, although Britain seemed harder hit.

The prime minister pointed to signs of economic improvement. Four years were not long enough, she said, to turn a country away from socialism.

At the end of May, Margaret Thatcher interrupted campaigning to participate in a summit meeting in Williamsburg, Virginia. Along with the leaders of seven other countries, she attended a service at the famous Bruton Parish Church, where, as a college student at William and Mary, George Washington had prayed.

These leaders discussed economic policies. Mrs. Thatcher told the press that the beginning of an economic recovery had been noted in all eight countries but that it would not happen overnight.

"There's no such thing as a quick fix," she said. "As we say, 'A quick cure is a quack cure.' "

Returning to England, Mrs. Thatcher plunged into the political battle. A bus was fixed up as a traveling office, and there her staff worked as they rolled from town to town. Denis went with her everywhere. He worried about her personal safety when in crowds of people, all of whom wished to shake her hand. Mark was out of the country, living in Dallas. He got home just in time to vote. Carol took an active part, later writing a book, *Diary of an Election*, in which she described in detail the punishing days on the campaign trail.

Mrs. Thatcher was not the only one trying to attract votes. All together there were ten parties that sent representatives to Parliament as a result of this election. These included the Scottish National with two winners, the Plaid Cymri (or Welsh National) also with two, and the Sinn Fein, an arm of the outlawed Irish Republican Army, whose single elected member did not take his seat in the House of Commons. It is interesting to note that no other country permits an outlawed organization to elect a member to its lawmaking body.

Parties that failed to win even one seat included the Ecology or Green party and the Communist party.

The three main political parties are the Conservative (or Tory), the Labour, and the Liberal parties. Since 1945 the Liberals have never had more than seventeen members elected to the House.

The Labour party is primarily a party of trade unions. In 1900, seven years after it was formed, a meeting was held with members of trade unions and socialist organizations to establish plans for labor to have representation in Parliament. It wasn't until 1918 that individual members were admitted. It is no wonder, then, that at party conferences, trade unions hold seven-eighths of the votes and are directly responsible for the choice of the party leader. This choice, of course, in a Labour victory at the polls, becomes prime minister.

Two unions were in the middle of their annual meetings the week of the election. Both decided to end their conferences early in order to release their delegates to campaign actively against the prime minister.

"Obviously, this will cost us money," one official said, referring to the cancellation fee for hotel reservations, but they believed it worth the financial sacrifice.

In the pre-election polls, Margaret Thatcher led. The London

Times claimed the Conservative candidates had a "patchy" record of working toward Mrs. Thatcher's objectives. The candidates' declaration that they intended doing so now had to be taken on trust. The editorial ended, "That trust exists almost solely in the personality and will power of the prime minister."

On election day, Mrs. Thatcher once more amazed even her closest friends and advisers by her stamina and energy. Up before 7:00 A.M., it was 2:00 A.M. the next morning before she learned she was returning to Parliament as Finchley's representative. She began her second term, she said, with a great sense of responsibility and humility.

At 3:50 A.M., on her way home from Finchley, she and Denis arrived at the Conservative headquarters. There she told her loyal workers, "We have to remember that all power is a trust and we must exercise it in that way."

At 5:30 A.M., she finally got to bed, only to be up an hour and a half later, at seven!

The Conservatives won by a landslide, handing the Labour party its worst defeat since 1922. All the grueling days of rushing to and from bus and plane and helicopter, of giving speeches in shopping centers and town halls, of shaking thousands of hands, had paid off for Margaret Thatcher.

She said, "It is all over now. The adrenaline is flowing. I don't know what we're going to do next. But don't worry. We are not going to call another election."

As laughter burst from the listeners, Denis piped up, "No, we are not!"

Clearly, the voters had told the prime minister they wanted more of the same. Exactly what was she doing that pleased them?

She had tackled three important domestic issues, each of which was a mainstay of the Labour party's doctrines. As prime minister, Mrs. Thatcher wanted to reverse the power of trade unions, return state-owned industries to private ownership, and offer tenants the opportunity to buy government-owned homes.

Perhaps the most surprising part of the election was the large number of trade unionists who voted Conservative. This confirmed her belief that her government's constant chipping away at the power of union leaders was popular with union members. She continued to do so.

Margaret Thatcher wanted to make sure that members had a voice in union affairs. Her government introduced to Parliament a Trade Union Bill that upset Labour members.

One provision made it illegal to strike without first holding a secret ballot of union members. Until then, voting to strike was done at an open-air meeting which frequently became rowdy. Tom King, Mrs. Thatcher's secretary for employment, claimed that a show of hands used in a closed, or 100 percent union, shop bullied people into voting to strike even if they didn't want to. This provision of a secret ballot to call strikes was to play an important part in the worst and longest strike in British history, the walkout called by the miners' union the next year.

Labour MPs fought against the requirement that unions with political funds must hold a secret ballot at least once every ten years to see if members wanted to continue the fund. This might in the future hit at the Labour party's financing, but Mrs. Thatcher believed that members should have a say in how their dues were spent.

Still another provision of the bill stuck in the throats of Labour MPs. It declared that a strike must be used in the interests of the workers and not for political party purposes, as had happened in the past.

The battle raged on the floor of the House of Commons. John Evans, an Opposition spokesman on employment, said during the debate in Parliament, "This bill removes the essential right of trade unions to determine freely the rules, Constitution, and procedures of their own organization."

John Smith, chief Opposition spokesman on employment, got cheers from Labour MPs by declaring, "When Labour returns to power, we will repeal the bill."

Some Labourites described it as a threat to democracy. Conservative Neil Hamilton said it was the first time he had heard giving votes to the people described that way!

The bitter debate continued, but in 1984 the bill eventually won enough votes to be passed into law.

On the personal side, on August 3, 1983, two months after the election, the prime minister had an eye operation. As people get older, a jelly in the inner eye contracts. This jelly usually sticks to the retina, but as it gets smaller it tears a hole. A previous unsuccessful attempt to seal the tear by laser had been kept secret.

The day after the operation Margaret Thatcher was walking in the hospital grounds and dictating letters. Denis told the press that hospital life was not to her liking.

"She'll be jumping up and down in forty-eight hours, that's for sure!" he added.

Among the many people who sent gifts were the queen and her mother, whose official title is the queen mother. Both sent flowers. Margaret Thatcher wrote her thank-you notes by hand, not only to them but to everyone who wished her well after her eye operation.

Although holidays always found the prime minister impatient to get back to work, she and Denis vacationed in Austria shortly after her eye surgery. In September, only one month after the operation, she spent thirty-six hours in Washington, D.C. There she received the Winston Churchill Foundation award and, once more, in the eyes of the Soviets, confirmed that she deserved the title "Iron Lady." Her talk, warning of the aggressive policy and power of the Soviet Union, seemed almost an echo of Winston Churchill's famous "Iron Curtain" speech on March 5, 1946, at Westminster College in Fulton, Missouri.

Margaret Thatcher greatly admired the United States. She has been accused of agreeing with the United States on some issues just for the sake of friendship. Even the London *Times* warned that the government's firm support of the United States left it open to the criticism that "Mrs. Thatcher is President Reagan's puppet."

Because the United States helped Britain during the Falkland crisis it came as a surprise to many people in President Reagan's administration when Britain refused, in October 1983, to join the U.S. invasion of Grenada, a former British colony. Indeed, one Pentagon official said there was a "deep sense of outrage" at Britain's attitude.

Instead of being congratulated for taking a stand against the United States' endeavor, the prime minister and her government were attacked in Parliament, not only by members of the Opposition but by Conservatives as well. She and her front-benchers were placed in a position of having to explain why they had not been able to stop U.S. troops from going to Grenada.

The closest Margaret Thatcher came to explaining the position of the United States was to say that a number of Caribbean states saw things in a very different perspective from the British, indicating that this time President Reagan agreed with the Caribbean people.

The year 1984 was just a few months off. It was to be a momentous time for Margaret Thatcher in her role of prime minister and for Margaret, human being.

Margaret Thatcher looks puzzled by a question from the press.

10

Nineteen eighty-four was a year of violence for Margaret Thatcher. This included violence due to the longest strike in British history, to the longest overseas problem in British history, and, on the personal side, due to her position as prime minister.

In March, Mrs. Thatcher faced a showdown with one of the largest unions in Britain. Prime ministers traditionally do not take on the unions in a dispute; they regard it as too dangerous political-ly. All of them want the thousands of votes that union members cast in an election. This gave union leaders a very powerful position for bargaining to get what they wanted from the government.

Other prime ministers may consider problems something to be avoided. Not Margaret Thatcher! According to John Newhouse, "Mrs. Thatcher attacked them as if she were leading a cavalry charge."

The government agency running the coal mines, the National Coal Board, announced that production needed to be cut by 4 percent. Approximately twenty mines would close and 20,000 miners would be left jobless, according to an estimate by the National Union of Mineworkers (NUM). That's all it took for Arthur Scargill, president for life of the union, to call a strike.

The mines scheduled to be shut were those losing money. In

Arthur Scargill's opinion, that was not reason enough. A "pit" that no longer yielded coal or had become dangerous should be closed; to him, those were the only acceptable reasons. The fact that about £1 billion—approximately $1.5 billion—of taxpayers' money was needed to keep these mines open made no difference to Mr. Scargill. The head of the Coal Board said that unions were not used to looking at the financial side of the business.

Unfortunately for Mr. Scargill, he had failed to get a strike vote from union members. That made his strike an illegal act.

Not all 180,000 miners went out; 40,000 miners continued to work. Some strikers soon returned to the mines. Mr. Scargill never had the complete backing of the membership, primarily because of his politics. He is a Communist. This caused many miners to doubt his motives. Did he really want to help them or was he more interested in overthrowing Margaret Thatcher's government?

His complete disregard for the law was upsetting to rank-and-file union members who were law-abiding people. Scargill sent flying pickets from one area to another. A flying picket is someone who pickets at more than one workplace. Called secondary picketing, this is against the law in Britain.

Two Yorkshire miners brought suit against Mr. Scargill and the NUM. He was served the legal papers called a writ, as he sat in the hall while attending the Labour party annual meeting that October. He and the union were fined for defying a judge's order to stop threatening nonstrikers. "A great and powerful union with large membership had decided to regard itself above the law," the judge said.

One of the miners, Ken Foulstone, told a press conference, "I feel very unhappy about having to take my own union to court to stop misuse of the members. But I feel the law of the land has been upheld."

As the strike dragged on, it developed into a contest of endurance between two very determined people, the prime minister and Arthur Scargill.

The union leader was a very personable man. "Arthur Scargill has a music hall routine," starts an article in the London *Times*, referring to his manipulation of the press. He turned the bias of the media into a grudging admiration for the "loner," for the man who took on the government. News shots of picket-line violence did not faze him. According to opinion polls, approximately one-third of the population sympathized with him.

He gambled on a coal shortage during the winter months, when the British Isles can get bitterly cold. The shortage never materialized; coal stocks plus some conversion to oil provided ample fuel.

The strike went on for a year with bitter feelings on both sides. Mr. Scargill accused the police of harassment; pictures of strikers' violence spoke for themselves. Before the men returned to work, fourteen hundred people had been injured and three people killed in actions directly related to the strike. Miners in Scotland and Wales demanded that those arrested for the violence be pardoned.

"Serious criminal acts have been committed," the prime minister told Parliament. "People who commit such acts must expect to face the consequences."

And when it looked as though Margaret Thatcher had become the first prime minister to win a major victory over a union, Mr. Scargill threatened, "Miners will now conduct a guerrilla war against the [Coal] Board."

When the strike ended with a ninety-eight to ninety-one vote by union delegates at a conference in March 1985, Mr. Scargill said, "We will guarantee that the dispute is to go on."

The workers did not return all at once; they drifted back to the mines over a period of time. To some, Mr. Scargill was a hero, Margaret Thatcher a villain. He had tried to save their jobs and had broken the law to help them. Many of the miners returned to work wondering how long their particular pit would stay open.

Ironically, by going out on strike and lowering the production of coal, the strikers gave the Coal Board what it wanted: less coal.

The pressures on the prime minister, especially during a time of crisis such as the coal strike, are enormous. No. 10 Downing Street is not only her residence; it is also her office. Was there any place she could go to "get away from it all?"

The answer is Chequers, a wonderful house set in the country outside of London in Buckinghamshire. It is owned by the government and staffed by members of the armed forces. Mrs. Thatcher has more of a chance there to relax than anywhere else. Her way of relaxing, of course, is to invite people to Chequers for lunch or dinner and carry on with business as usual!

She does invite personal friends, of course, but mainly the visitors are people connected with her career. It is a complete change for her, though, because all the housekeeping details are taken care of by the staff, who are devoted to her. And occasionally she takes a walk around the garden, something impossible for her to do in London.

At the same time that the coal strike was going on, Margaret Thatcher's government was proceeding with the "privatization" of other industries. This meant that the companies taken over by the Labour government were being returned to private ownership. (It wasn't until 1988 that returning coal to private owners was discussed in the newspapers.) Once, when Britain first began this policy of taking over industry, the British ambassador to Washington was asked, "What if, in the future, your country wants to return industry to private ownership; how will it be done?"

The ambassador answered, "Have you ever tried to unscramble eggs?"

He, of course, could not conceive of a Margaret Thatcher. She said, "Government ought not to run industry; they are not good at it."

One of the methods of returning a company to private ownership was to offer shares of stock in a company to its employees; any shares not purchased were then offered to the public. For example, consider the National Freight Consortium, Britain's largest freight hauler. When it "went private," 1,200 workers paid the equivalent of $1.50 a share. One year later, the cost of a share had gone up to $5.10. Of course, if the price of a share drops, then the worker will lose money. But National Freight's former workers, now owners of the company, admitted they turn off lights, don't waste supplies, and take better care of their trucks than they used to. "Repairs cost the firm money," said Curtis Small, one of the truck drivers turned owners.

The overall result has been an increase in productivity and a turnaround for Britain. Margaret Thatcher says she has turned "a lame-duck economy into a bulldog economy."

As prime minister, Margaret Thatcher changed the face of Britain in still another way. Feeling strongly that individuals, not the state, should own homes, she instructed her government to sell so-called Council homes, the British equivalent of public housing. Now, tenants had a chance to become owners.

This was not an original idea of the prime minister's. It had been tossed about since the 1960s, but no one had put it into practice. It proved one of her most popular policies, and seven years later, Margaret Thatcher enjoyed a ceremony that confirmed her belief that Britons want to own their homes. Alan and Ann Young of Forres, Moray, Scotland, became the owners of the one-millionth government-built home to be turned over to its tenants since Mrs. Thatcher inaugurated the policy in 1979. Happily, she personally handed them the keys—and a bottle of the prime minister's special whisky!

In the midst of the coal strike, back in October 1984, both major parties held their annual conferences. The Conservatives met at Brighton, a well-known seaside town. Their meeting was held in a nine-story Victorian hotel, the Grand. Margaret Thatcher was, of course, very active at the conference. On Friday, October 12, the prime minister worked late putting the finishing touches on her keynote speech for the next day. Finally, she thanked the two members of her staff for staying until the early hours of the morning to help and told them that they should go to bed as soon as possible.

That's what she intended doing. Then her principal private secretary, Robin Butler, said, "I know you're tired but there's one more paper you must do because they want the answer tomorrow."

So, with Denis sleeping in the bedroom next to the room she was using, Margaret Thatcher sat down to study the paper she had been handed.

On October 12, 1984, Margaret Thatcher escaped injury when a bomb exploded in the Grand Hotel, where she and other members of the Cabinet were staying.

"This is a day I wasn't meant to see."

11

Terrorism is a fact of life public figures live with daily. A sniper's bullet, a car bomb, a greeting that is returned by shots: there is no warning. And Margaret Thatcher was not exempted from terrorist designs.

At precisely 2:54 A.M., as Mrs. Thatcher started to read the paper handed to her by Robin, a bomb exploded in the Grand Hotel, a bomb that had been planted for the purpose of killing her.

The window and curtain of her room blew out into the street. Her first thought was of Denis. She headed for the bedroom but met him coming through the doorway. Police with drawn guns ran into her room, and more police arrived with Leon Brittan, home secretary, and Sir Geoffrey Howe with his wife, Elspeth. The Howes had the room next to the Thatchers' suite, Leon Brittan the other side of the Howes. Their rooms were more badly damaged than the prime minister's.

Margaret Thatcher described what followed: "The first instinct, I can tell you, when the bomb goes off, is to get close to an inside wall in case another one goes off, so immediately we all went into the corridor and into the room opposite to make sure the girls [members of her staff] were all right."

According to a policeman, the prime minister remained "icy calm throughout."

If Robin had not handed her that "one last paper" to read, she would have been in the bathroom, the room hardest hit in their suite.

Once more, Margaret Thatcher suffered the loss of valued friends through terrorists' actions. Four persons were dead; all had been active in Conservative party circles. A member of Parliament, Sir Anthony Berry, was one; another was Roberta Wakeham, wife of John Wakeham, a close adviser on whom the prime minister relied. John Wakeham was the last person to be pulled alive from the wreckage six hours after the explosion.

Even closer to her was a severely hurt couple, Norman and Margaret Tebbit. He was considered a likely successor to Mrs. Thatcher as leader of the Conservative party. The room he and his wife shared was on the floor above the Thatchers'. When debris burried Margaret Tebbit, her neck and back were injured; she may never walk again. Her husband, hurled from the third floor and trapped against a wall above one of the main exits in the hotel foyer, was discovered four hours later. Just his feet stuck out of the wreckage. Jokingly, he told the rescuing fireman, "Get off my bloody feet, Fred!"

One of those who rushed to help was Lady Airey, widowed by a terrorist's bomb five years earlier when her husband, Airey Neave, was killed as the result of terrorist action. Her room and the bomb were on the same floor, the sixth.

If the twenty-pound bomb had done maximum damage, almost all the British Cabinet would have been killed. As leaders of the Conservative party, they were attending the conference. The explosion had been, in Margaret's words, "an attempt to cripple Her Majesty's democratically elected government."

Much later, when asked if the bombing changed her attitude toward life, she said, "Oh, yes. It is infinitely more precious to me now. When something like that happens, it alters your perspective. You are not going to worry or complain about silly niggly little things any more."

The Irish Republican Army claimed responsibility. Their announcement ended, "Today we were unlucky. But remember, we have only to be lucky once; you will have to be lucky always. Give Ireland peace and there will be no war."

Margaret Thatcher responded by saying that all attempts to destroy democracy by terrorism will fail.

Who were these people who planted bombs that killed indiscriminately? What was so important to them that they committed such acts?

The Irish Republican Army (IRA) is an outlawed group whose members believe in using terrorism. Their goal is to get the English government out of Northern Ireland and unite their island into one nation.

The island of Ireland is divided in two: The southern portion consists of the Republic of Ireland, with a population that is 94 percent Catholic and 5 percent Protestant. It is an independent country covering 26,600 square miles on which 3,590,000 people live.

The other section, Northern Ireland or Ulster, is part of the United Kingdom of Great Britain with twelve representatives in the British House of Commons. Its population of 1,567,000 is 35 percent Catholic and 53 percent Protestant. Its area is 5,452 square miles.

The question facing the prime minister was, simply put, do the majority of people living in Northern Ireland have the right to decide who shall govern their section of Great Britain?

The position of the British government reflects the stand it has taken since World War II: The majority of the people of a country have a right to choose, and the minority, to keep the peace, must go along with the majority. If it does not, anarchy, or lawlessness, results.

The right of choice played a part in the Falkland war. It was the reason Prince Charles, the queen's son, handed the symbols of independence to the president-elect of Zimbabwe on April 18, 1980. It was the reason that India broke away from the British Empire and became independent on August 15, 1947. (The situation in India was similar to Ireland's in that two major religious groups existed, so upon independence, India was divided into two states, India and Pakistan.) The same holds true of other nations, such as the Republic of Maldives, the Kingdom of Lesotho (formerly Basutoland), and, on December 12, 1963, Kenya.

How could Britain do less for the people of Northern Ireland? The majority do not want independence; they do not want to be part of the Republic of Ireland. They want to remain part of Britain.

A large part of their desire stems from their religious preference. Most of the people in Ulster are Protestant, as is true of England; the population of the Republic is overwhelmingly Catholic. Religion and national interest are bound so tightly together that it is impossible to separate the two.

The history of the peoples of Ireland is a drama of tragedy and bloodshed that started centuries ago and continues to this day. There is no doubt about the cruelty and injustice that took place on that troubled island, some in very recent times, but remembering them does not put an end to today's brutalities, and that is what Margaret Thatcher has pledged herself to work for.

The centuries of misery of the Irish tenant farmer were not the fault of Margaret Thatcher, just as the Civil War and executions that followed the creation of the Irish Free State in 1921 cannot be blamed on the Republic's current prime minister. The two prime ministers have to accept the situation as it is and work from there for a solution.

These opposing views have turned Northern Ireland into a

scene similar to gang warfare. Following a period of relative calm, the IRA's terrorist arm, the Provisionals or Provos, stepped up its activities in the 1960s, 1970s, and 1980s. This was in response to the Protestants' rejection of an agreement for a Council of Ireland whose purpose would be to encourage cooperation between the two parts of Ireland.

The IRA Provos considered this a reason to launch new attacks against Protestants, and the Protestants responded by using the same methods. In 1972 the Provos shifted part of their campaign to the English mainland, where the attempt to kill Margaret Thatcher took place twelve years later.

In 1985 an agreement was made between the government of Margaret Thatcher and the Republic of Ireland. This called for a representative of the Republic to take a consulting role and be an official presence in Northern Ireland. The British House of Commons voted overwhelmingly—473 to 47—to approve the measure. So did the Irish Senate. There was even a meeting of the British and Irish Cabinet ministers, a giant step forward.

But the people affected the most, the Protestant majority of Northern Ireland, rejected the plan. They believed they had everything to lose and nothing to gain by this arrangement.

Is there hope for peace in Ulster? The atmosphere is changing as the governments of Britain and Ireland work for an equitable solution. If Margaret Thatcher as prime minister can find an acceptable solution to this ages-old problem, she will indeed have worked a miracle.

Reports of violence seemed to come to her daily. The Grand Hotel bombing took place in the middle of the coal miners' strike, and the violence that occurred during that dispute greatly upset Margaret Thatcher. She knew that other terrorists lurked in the background, ready to harm innocent persons.

London had had its share since she had taken office. Back in May 1980, gunmen had held hostages in the Iranian embassy. Again in September, twenty were held hostage at the same embassy while the gunmen demanded that ninety-one political prisoners in Iran should be provided with a plane and flown to London. In another incident, shots fired from the Libyan embassy killed a young English policewoman.

Margaret Thatcher and members of her Cabinet have been the targets of mail bombs, explosives sent in a letter that explodes when opened. Fortunately, no one has been seriously injured by them.

Often the IRA plants bombs around London. One in a car parked outside of Harrod's Department Store exploded killing five people. Another went off in Hyde Park where the Household Cavalry was parading, and a bomb exploded in Regent's Park when the band of the Royal Green Jackets was performing. A famous rifle brigade, the Royal Green Jackets had a battalion serving in Northern Ireland. In the latter two explosions, eleven soldiers were killed, fifty people injured, and seven horses died.

Margaret Thatcher was in the midst of planning a world tour when in November 1984 her schedule was interrupted once more by terrorism, this time thousands of miles away. Mrs. Indira Gandhi, India's prime minister, one morning walked in her garden and greeted those she thought were friends. They answered her "good morning" with shots, killing her. This occurred less than three weeks after the bombing of the Grand Hotel. At that time, Mrs. Thatcher had received a message from the Indian leader in which she wrote, "All terrorism and violence are condemnable and contemptible."

Security was beefed up to protect the prime minister, who dismissed the risks by saying they "are just something one lives with." Denis accompanied her to Mrs. Gandhi's funeral. On the plane flying home with them from India was Dr. Garret FitzGerald, then prime minister of the Irish Republic. He was an outspoken opponent of the IRA; he and Mrs. Thatcher had talked many times about the Irish question.

Six weeks after returning from India, Margaret Thatcher began a whirlwind six days with a visit from Mikhail Gorbachev, who had not yet assumed the Soviet leadership. She liked him immediately.

After their meeting, she boarded a plane that flew her around the world, spending a total of fifty-four hours in the air and traveling more than 20,000 miles. The main reason for the trip was the historic signing of the treaty with China by which the British gave up their possession of Hong Kong. She also visited Peking and Washington, D.C., with stopovers in Bahrain, Bombay, Guam, and Honolulu.

Once again, her stamina amazed those who traveled with her. Chris Moncrieff of the Press Association reported that she stepped from her plane looking as though she was returning from a week at the beach. The London *Times* claimed she showed the first sign of human frailty in that after her plane touched down, she did not dash off to the country but instead went to No. 10 Downing Street to snatch a few hours' sleep. After that, she drove down to Chequers for the Christmas holidays.

The year 1984 ended on a peaceful note for the prime minister after a very full twelve months. She spent the days with her children. But the memory of the bombing remained with her.

One beautiful day at Chequers, Margaret Thatcher was suddenly overcome with the realization of how narrowly she had escaped death.

With tears in her eyes, she said to her friends, "This is a day I wasn't meant to see."

Queen Elizabeth II and three former prime ministers join Margaret Thatcher in celebrating the 250th anniversary of No. 10 Downing Street as the official residence of Britain's prime minister.

*"It was to get that accurate infor-
mation to the public domain
that I gave my consent."*

12

Before scandal rocked the country in late 1985 and early 1986, Margaret Thatcher's days were crowded with the more usual events encountered by a prime minister. She did, however, travel a great deal more than other prime ministers had.

Before becoming party leader, her only trips outside the United Kingdom had been on her honeymoon to Portugal and Paris and for skiing trips in the Austrian Alps. The main criticism of her assuming the highest elected office in the country had been her lack of knowledge of foreign affairs.

Now she had become an acknowledged expert in dealing with other countries. Since 1979 she had journeyed around the world, including visits to such dangerous spots as Northern Ireland and a Palestinian refugee camp. Not only had her government successfully negotiated with China over Hong Kong, they had also arranged for the reopening of the border between Spain and Gibraltar, a diplomatic triumph.

On one trip to Moscow, Mrs. Thatcher was not so busy with world affairs that she forgot an old friend at home. Visiting a Russian supermarket, she personally picked out a can of pilchards (a fish whose young are called sardines) for Wilberforce, the resident tomcat at No. 10.

In fact, she was away so much in one year, 1985, the London *Times* ran two articles about her absences from England: one called, "Can Mrs. Thatcher Be Cured of the Foreign Bug?" and the other, "A Foreign Body at No. 10."

These trips are, of course, strictly business. They follow one another so quickly it was no wonder that on a visit to Indonesia Mrs. Thatcher made one of her rare mistakes.

At a reception at the British Embassy, the prime minister said, "We are all impressed by the way President Suharto and his cabinet are handling the problems of Malaysia."

Denis, who was standing next to her, whispered, "Indonesia, dear, not Malaysia."

She corrected herself and then said, "Thank you, dear," in what the London *Times* called a "frosty" voice.

Certain meetings, of course, she is expected to attend regularly, such as those of the European Economic Council, or Common Market. Then there are the economic summit meetings attended by world leaders of Western countries. Since her first at Williamsburg, she has not missed one. In this way, she has become acquainted with the heads of governments and learned firsthand how they handle problems in their countries. By 1987, when attending her eighth economic summit, she was the senior member, having been in office longest.

Other trips have a specific purpose, such as the one to China to sign the treaty dealing with Hong Kong. Another was the trip to the United States in February 1985. Mrs. Thatcher flew to Washington to urge President Reagan to do everything he could to make a success of the arms control talks with the Soviet Union he would be attending the next month in Geneva.

On this same trip, she accepted an invitation to speak to a joint session of the Congress of the United States. This presented a problem for Speaker of the House Thomas "Tip" O'Neill, an American proud of his Irish heritage. How was he going to introduce her? To be correct, he should call her "Prime Minister of the United Kingdom of Great Britain and Northern Ireland." It went against the grain for him to place any part of Ireland in the same category as England, Scotland, and Wales! He finally compromised by introducing her as "Prime Minister of Great Britain," ignoring Northern Ireland completely!

Wherever she went, her personal safety presented problems for the host nations. In Norway there were antinuclear demonstrations triggered by her visit. Norway has strict antinuclear laws, and feeling on this issue runs high. In Austria a bomb was found in the bathroom of a hotel in which she was to dine. Who planted it and why is still a mystery. Even closer to home, in Scotland where unemployment was exceedingly high, eggs were tossed at her car in an effort to let her know that her economic policies were unpopular.

Perhaps the safety issue played a part in the Thatchers' decision to sell their Flood Street home. It was located on a regular London street and had no protective devices. While they lived in the prime minister's quarters at No. 10 Downing Street, their Flood Street home had turned into a base for Mark on his trips to England from Dallas and for Carol, who was pursuing her journalism career at the *Daily Telegraph*.

But the Thatchers needed a home. Being prime minister is not a permanent job, and at any moment Margaret Thatcher might be challenged to a no-confidence vote in the House of Commons. If she lost the vote or the Conservatives failed to maintain a majority in the general election that followed, she and Denis would be required to move out immediately. In August, a seven-bedroom house on the exclusive Dulwich Gate Estate in South London became their new home.

High-tech security with cameras, a "panic button" to activate garden floodlighting, and electronic entry gates were part of the safety measures which undoubtedly appealed to the Thatchers.

Now, if an unexpected scandal—that horror of all modern politicians—brought down her government, she and Denis had a place to go that is safe.

Scandal had already marred her government. The most notorious one involved her trade and industry secretary, Cecil Parkinson, who had a love affair with his secretary, Sara Keays. In her story, published in a newspaper, the *Daily Mirror*, she claimed he was the father of her child. Because he was considered Mrs. Thatcher's favorite Cabinet minister and, at that time, the person most likely to succeed her as party leader, her firing him in 1983 took place amid much unfavorable publicity.

A scandal far more dangerous politically to Margaret Thatcher hit the headlines in 1985 and 1986. It started out as a routine matter. Britain's only manufacturer of helicopters, Westland, was bankrupt and planned to give, in exchange for financing, a small ownership interest to one of two competing groups. One consisted of five European companies which had gotten together for the purpose of bailing out Westland. The other, the United Technologies Corporation of America, included Sikorsky-Fiat (the Fiat Company is Italian).

Mrs. Thatcher and her trade and industry secretary, Leon Brittan, favored the Americans; Michael Heseltine, secretary of state for defense, adamantly supported the Europeans. Because the Ministry of Defense bought most of the helicopters, he believed he should have the final say.

Regardless of her feelings, Margaret Thatcher maintained that the issue must be settled by the Westland Board of Directors and stockholders, that the government must stay out of the decision-making policy, and, finally, that the matter really did not involve defense.

Mr. Heseltine was a colorful character nicknamed "Tarzan" by the media because of his unruly blond hair. He wanted to discuss the options at a full Cabinet meeting. He believed that as a minister of state he had a constitutional right to demand that the Westland affair be put on the agenda.

Margaret Thatcher had always considered the topics to be discussed at a full Cabinet meeting her choice and her choice alone. She refused to do as Mr. Heseltine requested.

Who was right? Because Britain has only an unwritten constitution made up of hundreds of years of tradition, policies, and laws, no one can say with certainty.

A Cabinet meeting was scheduled for January 9. Everyone hoped this would end the public squabbling between the two. After an hour, Mr. Heseltine stormed out and announced his resignation. It was the first time in ninety-nine years that anyone had walked out of a British Cabinet meeting. (That earlier one had occurred over the Irish question.)

So far, bad publicity and, according to the *Economist*, evidence of Mrs. Thatcher's increasingly cantankerous leadership had been the result.

But the worst was yet to come. The solicitor general (the equivalent of the attorney general in the United States), Sir Patrick Mayhew, wrote to Mr. Heseltine that he (Heseltine) had included some inaccuracies in a letter to one of the companies involved in the Westland competition. Sir Patrick's letter was leaked to the press, supposedly to embarrass Mr. Heseltine.

Forced to admit that her own office had authorized the leak, Margaret Thatcher found herself in the middle of a political crisis. She defended her action by claiming it was vital to give accurate information to the public because, she said, "we know that judgments might be founded upon that." She finally admitted, "It was to get that accurate information to the public domain that I gave my consent."

Never before had Margaret Thatcher come so close to being

forced to resign. People felt betrayed, for a large part of her popularity rested in their knowing she was straightforward, said what she meant, and was truthful. The Westland affair showed that she could be devious and calculating. Mr. Heseltine accused her of censoring Cabinet minutes and publicly announcing the government was staying out of the Westland decision making while actually backing United Technologies.

Finally it came to a showdown in the House of Commons. Once more, the Conservative majority stuck together to give a vote of confidence in her handling of the scandal. It was a narrow squeak, especially as she and her government had been very vocal about enforcing the Official Secrets Act, which included the leaking of documents, the very thing she had done!

Many believed that if Mr. Heseltine had not had such a weak case and had appeared more sincere instead of "playing to the grandstand" with his dramatic walkout, he might have gotten further in his attempt to unseat Mrs. Thatcher.

As late as October 1986, the threat of the Westland scandal still hung over Margaret Thatcher. During a debate over a committee report on it, a Labour MP, Tom Dalyal, said, "She is a bounder, a liar, a deceiver, a cheat, a crook, and a disgrace to the House of Commons!"

In the House of Commons, anything goes!

Other events had been taking place during the Westland scandal. Far more serious to England at large were the worst riots the country had ever suffered.

Rioting broke out in September 1985 in the Handsworth section of Birmingham, a large industrial city in the Midlands, or central area of England. More than half—58 percent—of the people living in Handsworth had been born outside the country. Most of these were either black or Pakistani.

A great many young people lived there; 46 percent of the population was under twenty-four years of age. In addition, over half the people had been out of work for over a year. Only 5 in every 100 black students leaving school the previous summer had found jobs. Handsworth rated as one of the most severely deprived areas in Britain.

The government, aware of the situation, gave Birmingham £82 million—roughly $102 million—in an effort to help the desperate, but it could not stop the pent-up feelings.

On September 10, when a police officer stopped a black man suspected of driving a stolen car, a crowd of black youths gathered. A small riot followed with three "bobbies," as the English call their police officers, injured. English police do not carry guns, although because of these riots, legislation is being considered to permit them to do so.

Two hours later, near the spot of the attempted arrest—the man got away—a fire started in a disused bingo hall. The fire officer in charge was approached by a black man who warned him not to put out the fire, that if his men did, trouble would start, and that is what happened.

Before the Handsworth riot ended, nearly 400 youths of all colors threw gas bombs, bricks, bottles, and everything they could find at the police, now wearing protective helmets and carrying shields. Shops were looted, cars overturned and set on fire, and people injured, some fatally.

Both drugs and insensitive policing were given as the immediate reasons for the riot; undoubtedly, the fact that Handsworth did not share in the economic prosperity that accompanied Mrs. Thatcher's programs in the south was largely to blame.

Rioting spread to other cities. In the Tottenham section of London, the violence ended with fifty-eight bobbies and twenty-four other people, including two children, injured and one policeman killed.

A high rate of unemployment continued to plague Mrs. Thatcher's government. New technologies were increasing the number of jobs in southern England, but in the north and in Scotland, jobs were hard to find. The Labour party believed this one fact alone would help put them back in power in the next general election.

But many events were to occur before the prime minister planned to call a general election. Her term still had approximately two and a half years to go. Before then, she would have to make many important decisions. One might even involve Great Britain at best in a series of violent terrorist acts and, at worst, in a war.

The question Margaret Thatcher faced was, should Britain help the United States launch an air attack against Libya?

President and Mrs. Reagan entertain Prime Minister and Mr. Thatcher at a formal White House dinner.

"There is an inherent right to self-defense."

13

"U.S. BOMBERS 'KILL 100' IN LIBYA RAIDS"

"'TAKE THAT!' SAYS THE PRESS AMID FEARS THE MAD DOG
   WILL BITE BACK"

"POLICE PUT ON ALERT FOR REPRISALS IN BRITAIN"

—London *Times*, April 16, 1986

In April 1986 Margaret Thatcher found herself once more embroiled in a heated discussion in the House of Commons. This time she was forced to defend her position in regard to Libya.

At 7:00 P.M. on the evening of April 14, United States Air Force planes had flown from American bases in England to bomb Libya. For the F-111s stationed there to be used on such a mission, it was necessary for the prime minister to give permission, according to the terms of the thirty-year-old treaty establishing those bases. Mrs. Thatcher did so. The object of this raid was an attempt to wipe out or severely damage Libyan leader Colonel Qaddafi's terrorist headquarters and camps, to "surgically remove," or at least lessen, the threat of terrorism.

The prime minister believed that this air attack was conducted under the terms of Article 51 of the United Nations Charter. This section states that if an armed attack occurs, self-defense is an "inherent right."

Did the term *armed attack* cover violence by Libyan-backed—or any other state-sponsored—terrorists? That was the key question. Mrs. Thatcher and President Reagan believed it did.

Back in 1969 Colonel Muammar Qaddafi had seized power from Libyan King Idria in a bloodless takeover. Since then he had established a nation that specialized in terrorism. The British and Americans became his prime targets, although he did not limit his terrorist attacks to them.

The list of deaths and destruction attributed to Libyan-backed violence increased. When machine gun bullets from a window in the Libyan embassy in London sprayed into a crowd of anti-Qaddafi demonstrators, resulting in fifteen injured and the death of a young English policewoman, Margaret Thatcher's government broke off diplomatic relations with Qaddafi's. Anger flared throughout the United Kingdom when the killer was permitted to return to his home with other members of the Libyan legation.

To the English, the supplying of arms to the Irish Republican Army was one of Qaddafi's worst crimes. Even so, Margaret Thatcher's government had never considered direct military action.

At the same time, relations between the United States and Libya had disintegrated rapidly following the burning of the U.S. embassy in 1979. In 1981 the Libyan embassy in Washington was closed by the United States government. The Reagan administration accused the Libyans of supporting international terrorism and concluded no improvement in relations was possible.

Both Mrs. Thatcher and President Reagan believed they possessed irrefutable proof that Libyan-backed agents had been responsible for a series of bombings. These included an explosion in a TWA plane en route from Rome to Athens in which four passengers, all American, were killed; a bomb that ripped apart a West Berlin discotheque, killing a U.S. serviceman and a Turkish woman and injuring 150 people; and the indiscriminate killings at the Rome and Vienna airports.

Margaret Thatcher told the House of Commons, "Terrorism thrives on appeasement. Of course, we shall continue to make every effort to defeat it by political means. But in this case, that was not enough."

The raid came as no surprise to Colonel Qaddafi. He had put Libya on an alert in case of such an attack, moving naval vessels to protected berths in Tripoli Harbor, flying most of his military aircraft to emergency airfields in the desert, and calling a medical alert in the hospitals.

The Soviet Union, Libya's ally, was notified by the United States of its intent. A Soviet warship, tied to a pier in Tripoli, put out to sea.

Margaret Thatcher faced a barrage of questions when she entered the House of Commons after the announcement of the United States' raid on Libya. Some people wondered if this might be the event that could bring down her government. An article in the London *Times* entitled "Lioness in a Den of Daniels" stated that "Every criticism from the Opposition bench was turned away with remorseless logic."

When asked why she had not urged President Reagan to go to the United Nations Security Council, she replied that the Security Council had already condemned terrorism and the condemnation had done no good. It could not take effective action to deter state-sponsored terrorism.

Referring to those killed, she said, "The casualties are, of course, a matter of great sorrow.

"We also remember with great sorrow all those men and women and children who have lost their lives as a result of terrorist acts over the years—so many of them performed at the Libyan government's behest."

Answering questions concerning other means of halting terrorism, Mrs. Thatcher stated, "The United States had asked Europe to take other action against state-sponsored terrorism. It asked for economic sanctions. It asked that we expel all Libyan People's Bureaus. Totally insufficient action was taken by Europe over the past many years."

When requested to tell President Reagan that United States bombers based in Britain should be used only for NATO purposes, she responded, "To leave a terrorist government sponsoring terrorism the world over secure in the knowledge that no other government would ever take any action or use the right of self-defense would be to increase the danger of terrorism."

An unanticipated backlash from Mrs. Thatcher's cooperation with the United States for the Libyan raid was the dramatic drop of 30 to 40 percent of American tourists to the British Isles. Fears of terrorist reprisals caused thousands of Americans to cancel their vacations at the cost of about £400 million (almost $600 million) in revenues to Britain.

Margaret Thatcher appeared on U.S. television in four interviews to urge Americans to spend their holidays in Britain. "The chance of your being hit by terrorism here is about the same chance as being hit by lightning," she told her TV audience.

In another interview she said, "Please come. Please change your mind." And in still another, "Life is normal. Come. We miss you."

For Mark Thatcher, the raid had an unexpected twist. Neighbors in his luxury high-rise in Dallas panicked at living in the same building, fearful that he might be a target for terrorist activities. He was asked to move out, which he did. He eventually settled in the fashionable Turtle Creek district.

In November, Mark made headlines again, this time by becoming engaged to a twenty-five-year-old Dallas girl, Diane Burgdorf, to whom he had been introduced by her father eighteen months earlier.

The Dallas press was amazed at the antics of the British news hounds in their attempts to discover details of Diane's life. The Dallas *Times Herald* said it was like "bloodhounds chasing a pair of East Texas possums." All they could uncover was that Diane had graduated from Southern Methodist University, had been a cheerleader, had come in second in a local beauty contest, and worked for a Texas bank and land developer.

Now thirty-three years old, Mark was a sales executive with Lotus cars. After their marriage early in 1987 the couple lived in Dallas. On February 28, 1989, one of Mrs. Thatcher's often expressed wishes came true when Mark and Diane had a son, Michael. The prime minister became a delighted grandmother.

At the same time, Carol's name also appeared in the news. A successful journalist, she had always been treated kindly by the media. Now the London *Times* headline read, "Carol Thatcher in row over newspaper job." She and Max Hastings, editor of the *Daily Telegraph*, gave different versions of what had happened.

The dispute centered over severance pay, which Carol claimed as her due when asked to leave. The editor maintained she had not been asked to leave but merely to switch from the features department to the editorial supplements. In December Carol left the paper "by mutual agreement" and became a free-lance writer.

Margaret Thatcher continued to be questioned about her part in the raid on Libya. Once she was asked if it might affect the outcome of the next general election. She did not answer directly but indicated she did not plan to call an election for quite some time. She said, "We can go all the way to June or July 1988. There are two years."

However, she changed her mind and scheduled a general election for June 11, 1987. It proved an excellent choice for the Conservatives: declining unemployment, lowered income taxes, increased private ownership of both homes and industry, and the limited power of trade unions created an atmosphere for not only making money but, for many people, actually saving it. Unemployment had not been eliminated, of course. It remained at 11 percent of the workforce, but the previous ten months had witnessed a decline in the total number of jobless persons.

The Labour party centered its campaign on Mrs. Thatcher's personality and style of government. It turned its electioneering into an assault against the prime minister and "Thatcherism," the name coined to cover her domestic policy. The Opposition called her an "ambitious would-be empress" surrounded by her "palace guard" and her "spineless doormat" Cabinet ministers.

Mrs. Thatcher's method of campaigning changed. Because of terrorist threats, she no longer could walk among the crowds, greeting supporters and shaking hands. The security risks to the prime minister were very real. Where she planned to stop to address a crowd was kept secret until 3:00 P.M. the day before and then told only to accredited reporters. Crowds were small because only loyal party members could be trusted. For the first time in British history, the prime minister had to rely on television to get her message to the voters.

Margaret Thatcher chafed under these necessary restrictions. In fact, whenever she spotted a group of people who appeared to be "ordinary" people and not handpicked, she excitedly broke into a run to talk to them!

She waged the battle to retain the Conservative majority in the House of Commons on the same philosophy in which she had always believed. The values she tried to instill in her countrymen were the same for her third campaign as for her first: anti-Socialism and a pro-property-owning democracy.

On election night, a bottle of champagne stood waiting for a victory celebration in the Thatchers' No. 10 Downing Street apartment. It was not on ice, for Margaret Thatcher is superstitious!

For the third time she led her party to victory, although the Conservative majority slipped to 100 seats. Her new term will be over in 1992. She is full of plans for these years. At the party conference in Blackpool in October 1987, she called educational reform the centerpiece of what is to be the "social affairs Parliament." She will concentrate not only on education but also on winning over to the Conservative party the last Labour party strongholds, the blighted inner cities. This means her government will give a financial boost to these depressed areas by improving both the environment and business prospects.

Will she run for a fourth term?

"Let's just see exactly where we get to," is her answer.

The champagne? In a victory toast, Margaret Thatcher, her family and friends drank it—lukewarm!

On June 14, 1989, Prime Minister Margaret Thatcher and President George Bush met at No. 10 Downing Street.

*"I had to come and feel the spirit
of Poland for myself."*

14

Returned to the job of prime minister for the third time, Margaret Thatcher showed the same spirit that had led her in her early political life to express publicly her beliefs on such explosive issues as immigration and the terrorist tactics of many trade union officials. She spent the remaining months of 1987 and the year 1988 fulfilling campaign pledges. By her actions, she managed to make people angry, pleased, and proud of her—all at the same time!

Her efforts to privatize industry, including the important steel industry, continued. The return of coal mines to private ownership with the miners themselves becoming part owners was promised for the 1990s. But the proposals to reorganize two traditional aspects of British life caused the greatest furor.

The first, the National Health Service, was one of the most important policies of the Labour government's welfare state. Since 1948, all Britons can receive medical service paid for by the government out of funds collected by taxation. It seemed to many that instead of reforming the system, the Thatcher government really intended to do away with government-paid health care. Under the new plan, patients will have greater freedom in choosing a doctor, and doctors will have a greater choice in picking a hospital or specialist a patient needs. Doctors and hospitals will be encouraged to advertise.

Critics fear that this is the first step in the commercialization of health care and that the poor will suffer the most. Margaret Thatcher maintains, "The National Health Service will continue to be available to all, regardless of income, and to be financed mainly out of general taxation."

The second plan of reorganization involved the legal profession. Although fewer people will be affected by changes in this area than by those in the National Health Service, the government's proposed overhaul has caused an uproar.

The legal system in Britain is two-tiered, composed of barristers and solicitors. In the United States, these are lawyers and they talk directly to clients and represent clients in court.

In Britain, it doesn't work that way. If a client of one of the 47,000 solicitors must appear in court, the solicitor locates a barrister to present the case in court. The new system will have a barrister or a solicitor do everything for a client, from discussing the case to appearing in court.

An important reason for the shake-up of the legal profession is to make British lawyers more competitive when the year 1992 arrives.

After two world wars, only twenty-one years apart, people began to dream of a United States of Europe. If all goes according to plan, 1992 will be the year when the dream becomes a reality.

As mentioned earlier, the first step was forming the European Economic Council to discuss trade. A meeting of the EEC was Margaret Thatcher's first official appearance outside of England after becoming prime minister in 1979. Since then, she has attended its meetings on a regular basis.

On January 1, 1958, the Treaty of Rome was signed, creating a European Community. At that time, Britain was not a member, joining the EC in 1970.

There are three governing bodies of the European Community. The Council of Ministers is the highest decision-making authority and is composed of the heads of member countries. The Commission makes recommendations to the Council as well as ensures that the rules laid down by the Council are carried out. The third governing body is the European Parliament. This is not a legislative body, such as the House of Commons in Great Britain or the United States Congress. Its primary purpose is to advise.

Margaret Thatcher firmly believes in the idea. From the beginning, though, she has pointed out the enormous problems and dangers to each country. One great worry is the elimination of all border controls. Drug dealers, terrorists, and criminals would be free to travel from one country to another, including the British Isles, without having to face any border inspections. Those in favor of opening borders claim that these undesirable people enter countries illegally now anyway.

The prime minister is against forcing nations to harmonize, or charge the equivalent amount, in sales and excise taxes. Also, Great Britain has quarantine regulations for pets entering the country. She fears that by letting up on Britain's requirements in order to harmonize with other nations, rabies could spread from contaminated animals in Europe to those in Britain.

The open-market plan appeals to everyone. Truck drivers will not have to spend time waiting in line to have documents checked at each border. Eliminating restrictions that increase prices will bring down the cost of various products. There are plans for one currency, one banking system, and one police force, but there is no guarantee that all these plans will be put into practice. A lot of work remains to be done.

She is also against a rule that the EC may tell British television companies when and how much time they may devote to advertising and that 60 per cent of the programs, not including news, sports, and game shows, must be made in EC countries.

But her greatest fear is that the European Community will become so powerful its rules and regulations will interfere with a large portion of her country's independence. If all twelve nations held the same political philosophy, that would be fine, but a variety exists. For example, the ideas of conservative Margaret Thatcher differ greatly from those of Jacques Delors, a French socialist who is head of the European Commission. Mrs. Thatcher firmly believes the only way to go is by "willing and active cooperation between independent sovereign states" maintaining free enterprise with a minimum of regulation.

Others who opposed many of the regulations remained quiet; Margaret Thatcher brought their fears into the open in a speech made in Bruges, Belguim, in September 1988. The German government dislikes the idea of a central bank. Germany's unionized workers are upset that their jobs will move to southern Europe where workers are paid less. Denmark, with high safety and health standards, worries they will be lowered by harmonization. France doesn't like tax equalization. Greece wants to maintain some border controls. Industry leaders in every country, including the United States, are afraid that the stiffer competition created by free trade after 1992 will put them out of business.

Many of her countrymen are pleased by the stand Margaret Thatcher has taken regarding the European Community. Almost all are proud of her for her actions in Poland.

"I had to come and feel the spirit of Poland for myself," the prime minister told Solidarity members who applauded her as she left St. Brygidas Church in Gdansk in November 1988. Dressed in a brilliant green coat trimmed in fur and a fur hat, Margaret Thatcher had a long talk with Lech Walesa whose leadership of Solidarity "has achieved so much," she said. Solidarity was an unofficial trade union which had been struggling for recognition by the Communist government.

The prime minister had been warned not to discuss Poland's

internal affairs. With her usual direct approach, she chose to ignore those instructions. At a dinner, she told the Polish Communist leader, General Jaruzelski, that he could expect little aid from the Western nations if he did not recognize Solidarity. The Polish people loved her!

It has been pointed out that in Britain she has been called a foe of trade unions, yet in Poland she supported one. Mrs. Thatcher has not been inconsistent. Her fight with unions at home has been with leaders who do not permit members a voice in union affairs. In Poland, she backed the workers' right to organize.

In 1987 protests were hurled at Margaret Thatcher for supposedly curtailing one of the basic freedoms, the right of free expression. Peter Wright had been a spy with MI5, the military intelligence section of the British government. He decided to write his memoirs. The Thatcher government was very concerned, for he might publish secrets that could endanger the life of others. The book *Spycatcher* was banned in Britain, although it appeared in other parts of the British Empire, such as Australia.

Later, there was no doubt as to how Margaret Thatcher regarded freedom of expression. When, on December 4, 1988, Britain reopened its embassy in Tehran after an eight-year closure, prospects were improving for the resumption of normal trade and diplomatic relations between the two countries.

Then a book was published in early 1989 that caused a split between nations that guarantee freedom of speech to their citizens and those that do not. Salman Rushdie, a Muslim born in India but a British citizen, is the author of *The Satanic Verses*, a novel that infuriated Muslims, who feel it is blasphemous and insulting to their religious beliefs. The Ayatollah Khomeini, then Iran's supreme leader, placed a death sentence on Rushdie. The Thatcher government whisked the author and his American wife into hiding. The twelve nations of the European Community recalled their envoys from Iran. The foreign ministers said they "remain fully committed to the principles of freedom of thought and expression within [their] territories." The United States agrees that no nation has the right to threaten the life of a citizen of another country.

Sir Geoffrey Howe, the British foreign minister, said that the book "is offensive about our government and our society and we resent that." He maintains that normal relations cannot be resumed between Iran and Great Britain until the death threat to a British citizen is canceled. On March 7, 1989, Iran broke off relations with Britain, and Britain expelled thirty high-security-risk Iranians.

In *The Satanic Verses*, Mr. Rushdie is very critical of Margaret Thatcher. It is ironic that he had to look to her government to protect his life, and she had to endanger her nation's relations with all Muslim countries to insure his freedom of expression.

In June 1989, President and Mrs. Bush visited England. Although the "special relationship" between the United States and the United Kingdom may not be as strong as it was during the Reagan administration, President Bush vowed that Anglo-American friendship "is continuing and will continue."

Their private talk, which lasted much longer than scheduled, included discussion of the sale of United States arms to Argentina, a sore point with the prime minister. She remains fully committed to the Falklands continuing as a British Crown Colony as long as the inhabitants desire. The British government is also concerned about the sale of missiles to Argentina by China. This has opened up fears that Argentina is once more planning an attack on the Falklands.

Another old worry that haunts Margaret Thatcher is the future of the people of Hong Kong. She believes that the best terms possible had been hammered out between her government and the Chinese in the agreement signed in 1984. Although a communist country, China has promised that Hong Kong's lifestyle will remain unchanged for fifty years. Freedom of speech, the press, association, travel, and religious belief is to be guaranteed by law, along with the right to strike. Also, the Chinese communist government pledged not to levy taxes! Then came the Chinese students' demonstrations in May and June of 1989. The severe crackdown by the communist government in China has caused many people to fear that it may not honor the agreement when it takes over Hong Kong in 1997.

In other parts of the world, sweeping changes have challenged communist authority. In order to avoid complete economic breakdown in Poland, General Jaruzelski and Solidarity reached a compromise, and in June 1989 the first free elections since World War II were held. As the first true opposition to a communist government, Solidarity won all 100 seats in the new Senate and 161 seats in the lower chamber. In August, Tadeusz Mazowiechi became the first Polish noncommunist prime minister in forty years.

This was just the beginning. By January 1990, all the countries of eastern Europe except Albania had challenged their communist leaders. In a dramatic move, East Germany demolished the Berlin wall and opened the door to eventual reunification with West Germany. Then came changes in the Baltic States and, most amazing of all, inside the Soviet Union itself. In early February, the Central Committee voted to give up the Communist party's monopoly on power, paving the way for a democratic multiparty system. Gorbachev, as president, was granted increased powers.

In 1992 Margaret Thatcher will be sixty-seven years old. A general election must be held then unless she decides to schedule one earlier. Her Conservative party may not win enough seats in the House of Commons for her to continue as prime minister. However, if she receives a majority from her constituents, she will still be a member of the House of Commons. Margaret Thatcher plans to remain in office far into the 1990s.

Prime Minister Margaret Thatcher posed for a formal portrait about the time she began her third term in office.

15

Margaret Hilda Roberts Thatcher: what is she *really* like? What impression does she give to the casual viewer? Is she always calm, cool, unperturbed, hair immaculate, clothes color-coordinated? How does she take criticism? How has she changed since becoming prime minister? These are some of the questions frequently asked about the prime minister.

Harold Goldberg, a Los Angeles businessman who saw her walking across the tarmac at the Manchester airport, enthusiastically exclaims, "Vibrant! She is vibrant!"

That part of her personality does not come across in still photos or on television. Instead, she appears unruffled and very much in control, almost as though she were emotionally cold.

Yet she has cried in public, especially when under great personal stress. When Mark was missing in the Sahara and at the graves of those killed in the Falklands, her restraint broke down, revealing a side usually buried deep within her.

More surprisingly, her temper has flared in public, to the delight of the press. At times she has been infuriated at some remarks of Prince Charles, the queen's oldest son and heir to the British throne, when he seemed to be critical of her government.

Also revealing have been her relations with the ministers of state in her Cabinet. From the beginning she has been criticized for her behavior at Cabinet meetings. It is rumored that she is rude, scornful, and unreceptive to new ideas. A great many Cabinet ministers have resigned or been fired, usually with bad feelings. They, having moved to the back bench in the House of Commons, might start a "palace revolt," which could finally cause the end of Margaret Thatcher's government. For example, the London *Times* called her "careless" in 1988 for falling out with the "most successful chancellor of the exchequer," Nigel Lawson, "in living memory." He did, however, weather the storm and remained in her Cabinet until October 1989.

Those who work most closely with her, her staff, are devoted and find her thoughtful; ministers in her government find her difficult, haughty, stubborn, and demanding. The greater the success of her policies, the more impatient she becomes with those who oppose her. These characteristics have always been part of her disposition; they just show up more often as time passes.

A standard joke since she took office has been that the prime minister would like to fill all the Cabinet jobs herself!

No matter what her mood—tearful, angry, pleased, or impatient—she always conveys the same immaculate impression. One of her critics blames her for her neat appearance on television shortly after the Grand Hotel explosion when others were shown still in their robes and hair disheveled. She, of course, was still working and had not been to bed.

Her hair is set twice a week. Frequently, on those hectic jet trips, she sees to it herself. On one visit to Saudi Arabia, she and Carol, who accompanied her, blew the lighting system in the palace at Ar Riyadh by plugging in Mrs. Thatcher's heated hair curlers!

Her style of dress has changed. No longer does she wear frills, bows, and fussy necklines. She has switched to collarless suits, creating a business executive image—and a tough one at that! But always around her neck is a two-strand pearl necklace, a long-ago gift from Denis.

Although a variety of opposition to Margaret Thatcher exists, everyone likes her husband. Denis is considered the ideal husband for her. Immensely proud of her, he is content to remain in the background. Now retired, all he asks is to be free to play golf, although he is never far from her side on trips, campaigns, or meetings. Incidently, she still fixes Denis his breakfast at 7:30.

She trusts his judgment. Once he sat quietly in a hotel room for hours while his wife and her writers wrote, rewrote, and re-rewrote a speech she was to make the next day. In the early hours of the morning, he suddenly said, "That's it." Margaret Thatcher delivered the version of the speech Denis had approved!

Not all women admire her. Not forgetting her famous remark about asking a woman if you want something done, she had nonetheless appointed few women to important positions in her government. Urging her to impress upon her ministers that they should listen to women, Labour MP Harriet Beckham said, "Women make up more than half the population, yet Mrs. Thatcher clearly thinks women do not have much to offer."

Early in her third consecutive term as prime minister, Margaret Thatcher was sharply criticized for the way she reorganized her Cabinet. It was well known that Sir Geoffrey Howe, foreign secretary for six years, opposed some of her policies on the European Community. In July of 1989 Mrs. Thatcher replaced him with John Major, a junior Cabinet secretary with no foreign policy experience, and Sir Geoffrey reluctantly became deputy prime minister. The manner in which she made these and other changes caused an uproar. In October the prime minister moved Mr. Major from foreign secretary to chancellor of the exchequer after the unexpected resignation of Nigel Lawson. He and Mrs. Thatcher had not agreed on how quickly Great Britain should tie its monetary system to the proposed common currency of the European Community.

After more than a decade as the most powerful person in her country and one of the most powerful in the world, Mrs. Thatcher remains true to the beliefs she took with her when she left Grantham for Oxford: hard work, serious study, doing for oneself, and doing one's duty. And add to that, doing what she believes is best for Great Britain.

President Bush toasted Margaret Thatcher at a dinner as one who "hold the reins of history." An assessment of her role in British history—indeed, in world history—is impossible at this moment. It will be from a vantage point in the future that her life story and its impact on her times can be told. Then, in that distant future, those hidden characteristics and secret thoughts that make up a person may have surfaced from letters she has written and from notes she has made.

Perhaps, when she finally steps down from her position of power, she may write her autobiography. If she does, it will be an important contribution to understanding not only British politics but also this woman who, by her active part in British government, truly belongs to history.

Further Reading

Books

Current Biography, W.H. Wilson Co., New York, 1975.

The Europa World Year Book 1989, Volume 1, Europa Publications Limited, 18 Bedford Square, London, WC1B 3JN, England, 1989.

Gardiner, George, *Margaret Thatcher*, William Kimber, London, 1975.

Garfinkel, Bernard, *Margaret Thatcher*, Chelsea House, New York, NY, 1985.

Harris, Kenneth, *Margaret Thatcher*, Little, Brown & Co., Boston, MA, 1988.

Hughes, Libby, *Madame Prime Minister: A Biography of Margaret Thatcher*, Dillon Press, Minneapolis, MN, 1989.

Junor, Penny, *Margaret Thatcher, Wife-Mother-Politician*, Sidgwick & Jackson, London, 1983.

Mayer, Allan J., *Madame Prime Minister*, Newsweek Books, New York, NY 1979.

Morris, Brian, Peggy Crane, and Klaus Boehm, *The European Community*, Indiana University Press, Bloomington, Indiana, 1981.

Murray, Patricia, *Margaret Thatcher*, W.H. Allen, London, 1980.

Paxton, John, *A Dictionary of the European Economic Community*, Facts on File, New York, New York, 1977.

Thatcher, Carol, *Diary of an Election*, Sidgwick & Jackson, London, 1983.

Periodicals

Barron's, "The Miner vs. the Iron Lady" by Andreas Whittam Smith, October 15, 1984.

Britain's System of Government, A Central Office of Information reference pamphlet, No. 21/86.

British Heritage, "The Palace at Westminister" by Lord Crathorne, December/January 1987.

The Economist, January 18, 1986; February 1, 1986; October 10, 1986.

Good Housekeeping, "Margaret Thatcher's Life Story" by Douglas Keay, April 1985.

Insight, "The Iron Lady's England," December 14, 1987.

The New York Times, various articles.

The New Yorker, "Profiles: The Gamefish" by John Newhouse, February 10, 1986.

Newsweek, March 18, 1985.

Organisation of Political Parties in Britain, A Central Office of Information reference pamphlet, No. 174/84.

Paris Match, article by Carol Thatcher, January 22, 1988.

The Times, London, numerous articles.

The Wall Street Journal, various articles.

Index